INDEX

Nathan Coppedge

2

HOW TO BE SMART

Nathan Coppedge

This text is designed to help with intelligence. However, I cannot promise an immediate gain in I.Q. I can only promise engaging material which I hope will be sufficiently stimulating.

HOW TO BE SMART

Basic Brain Functionality:

1. First, stop feeling like cotton candy unless it helps.

2. Second, make sure the parts of your brain are not attached to poodle positions, but are rather condensed inside your head. If you feel like a devil, melt the imaginary horns into a brain.

3. Then, stop trying to excrete your brain. Let it perform.

4. Now, let your brain naturalize itself with images it identifies with, such as a lake, or hearing chimes, or thoughts about music. Think of it as flexibility—plasticity.

5. Read until you are fluent and somewhat literate in at least one language.

6. Practice writing.

7. Learn symbols. Even make some of your own.

8. Learn how to add, subtract, multiply, and sometimes divide small numbers. Learn to use variables with this process. Learn how to use exponents and roots. http://www.nathancoppedge.com/mathematics.html

ADVANCED:

1. Think, don't think about brains.

2. But if you do, consolidate to variables which stick close by. You don't need to inflate anything.

3. Now you can 'focus' your thoughts.

4. Or explore a small area, like a memory temple.

MEMORY TIPS:

1

Remember the important parts.

Make a list of the parts that are most complex and hardest to remember in abbreviated format.

Now, assuming you have basic knowledge of the subject, studying the complex parts until you have key intuitions about them will help greatly for your exam.

2

Study more intensively (on the parts that are important).

3

Develop networks of association.

Remember patterns in association.

4

Keep an active memory.

HOW TO BE SMART #1:

THE CALCULUS

Differential Calculus, (Part I.)

Calculus is stupid. Calculus is for extroverts. It's either totally easy, or you learn calculus. Calculus is about thinking —- wait that's for philosophers.

The origin is a variable. The derivative is the angle of a line —- that's a small thing somehow, however, isn't it? The process might be unlimited. Even the opposite mathematics has its limits. It also may have no function. There are no opposites in calculus: there are only functions. Structures are imaginary. Applied calculus is the tough part—for which you have your handy calculator.

You can't be on the side of calculus—- Calculus just IS. One thing to know is that calculus always has a power. If you input zero you get zero, just like in algebra.

Advanced concepts in calculus:

1. Everything of value is outside calculus.

2. Maybe +3.

3. Calculus for all integers.

That's just an idea.

It's arbitrary in God's logic is one of the first things I learned. Even now in calculus there is a division between professors who teach calculus as intuition and those that teach it as pure mathematics. Ultimately there may be more than one way to do calculus but remember, calculus is stupid , or you're a genius.

Towards the end of his life, Leibniz lamented: what's human about calculus? So, calculus does have a downside. I'll leave that as a puzzle.

Concluding Remarks of the First Lesson

Sometimes we think calculus is a disease. Sometimes we think it is not logical at all. But mostly we think it is a highly useful thinking tool. Perhaps you'll side

with the Leibniz who thought it was in-
human, or perhaps you'll side with the
Leibniz who brought it upon himself to
invent calculus.

Integral Calculus (Part II.)

Wrong! Doubly wrong! Specifics don't
matter. Form a hypothesis, then throw it
away! Apply the existing hypothesis, be
conventional. Get it right! It concerns science! Be scientific! Clouds are clocks!
Simplify always! Stay distanced from
your
work. Or pull an Einstein. Know. Philosophy is contraband. The rest is history.

ADVANCED CALCULUS

Posterior Calculus (Part III.)

Now, I told you it wasn't about philosophy, but it is! All you need to know at
first is Delta V. Whatever you interpret
from is analytic a posteriori. Because you
know you will get what results—- You
have to begin somewhere, so you begin

with the effect of an unseen cause. The cause is analytic. Delta V. is when you attach an effect to a cause—-And you call it —- what do you call it? Analytic. The rest is logic… I'm sure you can figure it out. It depends on the case.

Applied Calculus (Part IV.)

Advanced calculus, also called applied calculus, is summarized by a particular range of modes or conceptual functions:

Range: "And other languages besides English" (extending the function).

Importance: Bounded or Unbounded, Finite or Infinite.

Definition or No Definition.

Conditions or Laws (parameters).

Identity: special function or no special function.

Creativity: "Unless we change the function".

Now a concluding remark we might owe to Immanuel Kant:

"For every dupe there is something doubtful...
For every doubt there is something dutiful."

CALCULUS!!!

EXTENDED CALCULUS

Coherent Calculus (Part V.)

Where sums are coherent, they add up to zero relative to the origin.
They become transparent.

Coherent limit X = indefinite integral of F (θ) dx

Where $\theta = \Delta\, d\,(x, y, z)$

$\Delta\, d\,(x, y, z) + \int f\,[\Delta\, d\,(x, y, z)]\, dx$ = coherent calculus for 1-d.

Maybe quadratic ally / categorically

Seeing this to be somewhat relative,

Δ d (x, y, z)

OR / AND

$\int$ f [Δ d (x, y, z)] dx =

Coherent calculus:

$\approx \int$ f [Δ S] dx

S = mod dx
Parts and wholes.

$\approx \int$ f [Δ mod d(x)] dx

= opp (parts and wholes) parts

(CONTINUED BELOW…)

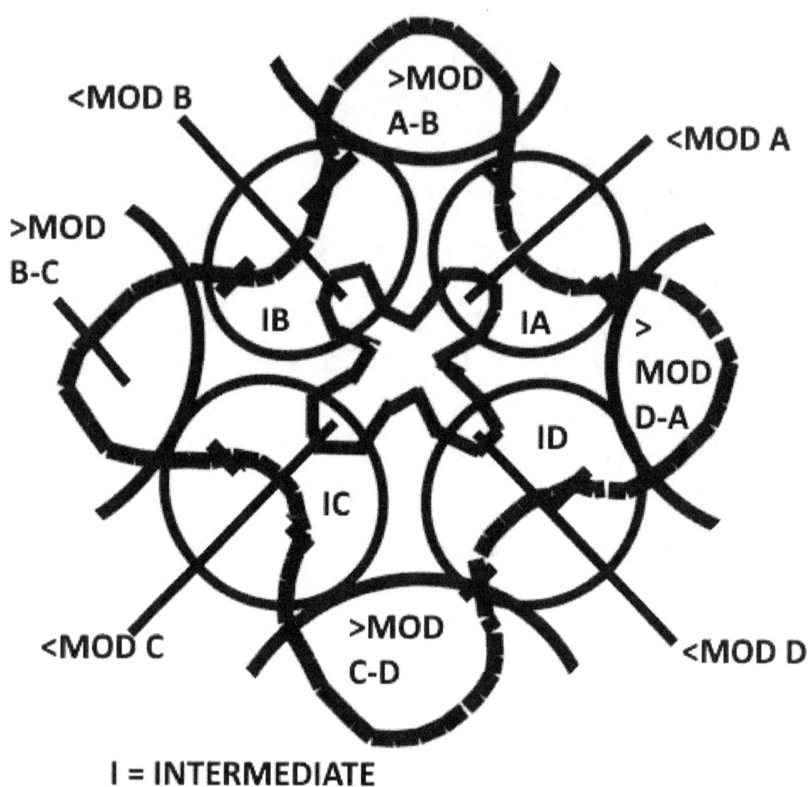

< ½ mod = axial whole = whole part (x, y, z) axial

> ½ mod = part-whole opposite = +dimension

Rationicitation of intermediates.

Quasi-rationals (between coherent and variablistic).

Symbolic corollary sought.

What is done on the inside is done reverse on the outside. Outside defines how significant the inside is. If there is no inside or outside it is all f (q). Inside is the coherent +dimension. Outside is the coherent whole-part (x, y, z).

Between >mod D-A and > mod A-B is intermediate A, which is coherent A.

Between >mod A-B and >mod B-C is intermediate B, which is coherent B.

Between >mod B-C and >mod C-D is intermediate C, which is coherent C.

Between >mod C-D and > mod D-A is intermediate D, which is coherent D.

<mod A and <mod B = intermediate A - intermediate B.

<mod B and <mod C = intermediate B - intermediate C.

<mod C and <mod D = intermediate C - intermediate D.

<mod D and <mod A = intermediate D - intermediate A.

Logic operation…

Where d = dimensions,

And t is an as-yet undeclared time variable or morphism,

$$|[\ \ \text{logic } t \approx \text{correlative } \Delta \ d \ \ ]|$$

Coherent calculus = logic t correlative Δ d

e.g. if d = 3, {[(b2 - b1) + (c2 - c1) + (a2 - a1)]

- [(a2 - a1) + (b2 - b1) + (c2 - c1)]} * logic t = coherence.

Unless the logic is dimensional, it all reduces to logic.

Depending on how you treat the matrix of numbers, other formulas may also apply. For example, perhaps the matrix involves subtraction, or perhaps the matrix involves a specific form of logical differentiation such as categories. In each of these cases, what modifies the value is either morphism or logic, and otherwise, dimensional logic.

General Calculus (Part VI.)

Inspired by previous works, such as
Clues About Coherent Calculus and System 2, I set about to design a concept of
multiple-calculus or polycalculus.

An initial clue is that polycalculus relates
to 'many worlds' of calculus. This could
be equated for example, with adding sig-
mas.

Another interpretation is that other logics
could be used which are less about sums
and more about modifications between
perspectives. Although some of these
would produce a perspective that is pro-
noucedly linear, others would produce
differentiation or layers that may be either finite or infinite.

Thus, initially three categories exist: non-
valued, quantitative, and infinite. In a
wider sense, the system also accepts
modifications of these. So, for example,
quantitative could become arbitrary, ambiguous ... number theory. Non-valued
could be evaluative, transitional, physical... etc. Infinite could have a qualified

or unqualified standard.

The question becomes, how to make math out of all this? In one sense the outcome might be irregular and disorganized. In another sense it might be structured by the involved elements.

Physics... number theory... qualified or unqualified appears to be the linear, quantitative approach to polycalculus. This assumes some slant towards coherence.

However, we can add to this concepts which extend the method and permit greater control of the results:

Symbols... physics... number theory... unqualified... qualified...set theory... megaverses...

For better use, we might seperate these into pairs:

1. Symbolic physics.
2. Unqualified number theory.
3. Qualified set theory.
4. Megaverses.

At this point it should be possible to grasp something of what is meant by polycalculus: A branching structure taking a wide variety of well-chosen operators, in which the expression of the result is open-ended, and may begin or end in multiple places and for multiple purposes, always incorporating some of the above elements.Thus, polycalculus can be simple or complex, parsimonious or ersatz, symbolic or naive, rigorously mathematical or even be a single logic operator. There is nothing about polycalculus that makes it inherently organized or rigorous, except that it's structure provides a general format for finding (with some effort) all forms of calculus.

See also later developments: First Investigation Into A Major Class Theory of the Polycalculii

Michael's Calculus (Part VII).

Calculus --> (Preamble) --> Mathematicians think they're right but they're always wrong --> There's nothing left except to not be right, except to be 'wrong'. Wrong qualified this way is really right, but will never (except rarely) admit it.

Examples:

We're trying to be fair (integrate) -->
(mathematicians are always right) -->
Mathematicians are almost always right,
but this time they're wrong --> If we integrate, it will disintegrate. This is a disas-
ter. We have to accept the information as
we find it.

Now we have a new function to map out
--> (What are we going to do?) --> We
can't try mathematics. We already tried
that if we know what we're doing. -->We
can do something new with mathematics.
Something creative and original. It
sounds hopeless. So we just give up, and
work where we started.

Now, there's something wrong with our
data. The equation doesn't match up -->
(Is there something wrong?) --> The math
can't be wrong unless there's something
wrong with the data, right? Wrong! The
math can be wrong! --> Well, we can't
start over. We have to accept part of the
equation is right, because if it's wrong,
it's the data that's wrong. But, we must
admit, we were completely wrong! That's

how to be right.

The formula works! Then how did we get it right? --> (Have we thought about this before?) --> We got it wrong A LOT OF TIMES! Remember, mathematicians are always wrong! --> So, this time we got it right! So what! Now we are a mathematician, and now we have to be very careful. We are now fully responsible for everything we do! This is calculus! Sometimes its wrong to be right! You have to feel wrong to get it right!

NOTE: This writing is designed to teach "The Intuitive Calculus" and hopefully will jump-start knowledge of calculus, but is BY NO MEANS a standalone guide to calculus. Ownership and use of a textbook as well as academic instruction are critical expectations in developing a real knowledge of calculus, and the significant algebraic and trigonometric aspects have been glossed over in this writing. Hopefully this will make the "Intuitive Calculus" easier to grasp at every level of education than most academic treatments of the calculus, however similar they pretend to be to the Intuitive Calculus.

HOW TO BE SMART #2
PHYSICS

I. NEWTON'S LAWS OF MOTION

An object in motion tends to stay in motion.

Every action has an equal and opposite reaction.

Motion continues unless there is resistance.

These laws continued to be seen as having universal relevance until Quantum Mechanics came along, and determined the laws to be different at different scales. Nonetheless, Newton's Laws of Motion tend to remain accurate at what we call intermediate scales, or some say, above the atomic level.

II. THE LAWS OF THERMODYNAMICS

0: That, all conditions being equal, energy remains constant.

1: That, with some resistance, energy decreases.

2: That, with heat energy, energy tends to dissipate.

3: That, since most structures have some void, no perfect seal can be built to contain heat.

4: That, over infinite time, energy tends to return to zero.

5: That energy tends to be created from the destruction of particles.

**These may not be the official definitions, but they give an clear
overview of the types of concepts covered by Thermodynamics.**

III. ADVANCED PHYSICS

A black hole is a singularity.

You don't know your wave functions if you don't know that.

A black hole is a hole: an absence of space relative to time.

Heat is a bowshock, the wave of a crescendo.

Waves describe everything in motion, if it is also admitted a wave can also be a surface.

Quanta describe particles at rest.

The foundational principle is construction and continuation.

But this basic principle is broken by indefinite energy states.

Wave-particle duality is broken by a further principle of the multiplication of elemental composite properties resulting from indefinite energy.

Many of the correlated properties concern either waves or composite properties, such as those observed in material science and biology.

If there are unique or unusual properties, they tend to emerge because of an opposition singularity or some of the properties mentioned above.

Physicists say that an oppositional singularity is not a black hole, but people don't listen.

In fact, an oppositional singularity is any state involving sufficiently opposite properties which might create a unique energy state.

IV. STRING THEORY

When I learned the basics of calculus, I also learned how to have insights into string theory. My first idea was the equal-energy particle theory = string theory, which at least sounds similar to other string theories.

From the theory of equal energy, we can get concepts such as supersymmetry, singularity, and virtual singularity (informational vectors), which suggests that the theory actually is a form of string theory, although perhaps a misguided one.

V. SCHRODINGER'S EQUATION

$$i \text{ Heisenberg vector } \frac{\text{integral}}{\text{integral } t} \text{ X Psi}$$

= Total Heisenberg energy Psi

The h with the raised bar means total entropy. Heisenberg can
be understood as energy cancellations. The small h with the cross means
energy moment. The rest says that the observable energy at-moment
equals the total observable entropy! Do you see what it is? It's how fusion reacts! It's the behavior of pure nuclear energy! (The double integral
means the energy is conserved
relative to energy).

VI. EIGEN FUNCTIONS

Sigma Sigma.

I grasped something.

There are n-sides to that coin.

It's called complexity.

HOW TO BE SMART #3

--MEDICINE--

HIPPOCRATES

"Life is short, and Art long; the crisis fleeting; experience perilous, and decision difficult. The physician must not only be prepared to do what is right himself, but also to make the patient, the attendants, and externals cooperate."

—Hippocrates

Section 1.

Study Chinese medicine (carefully), don't grow old.

Patients can be controlled (and helped!) by food, psychologically.

Section 2.

With sleep and onset, expectations are neither more nor less than is normal.

Avoid toxicities.

Good food is simple.

Serious patients recover.

There are signs with recovery.

Recovery requires belief.

The onset of illness must be carefully watched.

Patience is frequently the best cure.

Section 3.

Humans are not always apt to adapt, and they are more adapted to cold than heat.

People suffer the maladies of their age in life.

Section 4.

Become accustomed to the ugliness of medicine.

Disease has perplexing cases which are more subtle and generally less extreme.

In extreme cases watch out!

Section 5.

Have a healthy fear of death!

Sexy people reproduce.

Section 6.

Watch out for peculiarities; the cause may
be something deadly.

Death is common or inevitable; immortality is rare or inexorable.

There are things worse than death.

Section 7.

Discoloration is unhealthy.

Good from bad is good, but bad from
good is bad.

Good never comes from bad, although bad
can come from good.

THE PHYSICAL DOCTOR

You want to make accurate predictions that stear you in the direction of good health.

2. The prediction can be that sports are hard.

3. You need to do the necessary training.

4. Your neck gets sweaty, your palms get wet, you work up adrenaline.

5. Then what? You feel hungry. You might eat too much.

6. You need to eat healthy unless you plan to work out when you're 80.

7. Nuts and fruit is the way to go, and a few carbs, and meat if you're really hungry.

8. Plenty of fluids.

9. Avoid artificial sweeteners and other artificial additives that sound like benzohydrate and Yellow 40.

10. The ideal diet also includes some herbs, and a little bit of protein. And plenty of veggies if you can stand it.

11. Avoid salad dressing, fat, and sugar.

12. Eat only when you feel hungry. Don't eat excessively, eat for nutrition, when you feel hungry.

PHILOSOPHY OF GENERAL MEDICINE

Things don't look good.

Then they must already be bad.

We must cause an improvement.

Otherwise, it is not good.

The first to be ill:

1. May be very rich.

2. May have a cure to their own problem.

3. It may be difficult to treat them.

But the big picture is different:

1. There are long-lasting effects.

2. What is being expressed is an otherwise-unknown aspect of disease.

3. The cure is the soul of the patient.

Thus, it is money well-spent, considering the variety of disease, and the full scope of the problem rarely becomes clear.

MITHRADOTALISM

Note: This is NOT part of the Coherent Knowledge series, OR an attempt to persuade anyone to try poisons. I will clarify my intentions soon.

I have come across the expression 'course of disease' and my theory is it was originally proposed by Mithradates (in Latin, presumably).

This angle sheds new light on what is meant by medicine, almost in general. For clearly what Mithradates meant by 'course of disease' was some form of Mithradotalism.

But what was the meaning of this? Clearly, for one thing, what was meant was that "disease is the source of the cure". For example, a mental disease could be cured by becoming a genius. A physical disease could be cured by continuing exercise, etc. That is at least what I think he meant by 'course of disease'.

But I think he also meant a particular psychological attitude, an emotion of moderation. I have seen the effects of this approach myself in curing stomach complaints.

A mere attitude shift can change the entire course of disease. One moment I think I have pancreatic cancer, and the next minute I feel normal. What could explain this?

Well, I attribute the effect to the emotion of moderation, which is really the effect of Mithradotalism related to Mithradates's concept of 'the course of disease'. I would not be surprised if this factor is an active part of the psycho-physiology of centenarians.

WRITING LIKE A DOCTOR: TEMPLATE FOR MEDICAL WRITING

How To Write similarly to the Annals of Medicine.

1. Incident of the report. In reference to. Background theory of the notation. (Note of acumen).

2. Ellucidation: Scope, Reason, Integration.

3. Question of interest (a leading question). Deeper clarification. Often followed by proverbial cases, conventional case examples illustrating medicine. Tie-in with medicine or note of acumen.

4. Continuation with broader scope (psychology, biology), with strong hint of integration. Personal experience.

5. Heavy proverb of medicine. Acme of disease. Mysterium, Ask what would explain this.

6. Illustrative of the whole case (the point you're getting to, particularly using hint of integration and weight of evidence). It is the incident of the insight. A final brilliant point applicable to future cases.

HOW TO BE SMART #4
PHYSICS & MATHEMATICS

I finally cracked the meaning of some of the notorious formulas of science! Maybe you can learn from me!

First: 1. Science is not so different from philosophy, and 2. If you know that, it can be fun, but it requires some thought!

I found an image on Pinterest (Ten Equations that Changed the World from Futurism.com) that put some things together for me. What I noticed is all the equations are supposed to be important and blindingly obvious.

I won't cover the harder equations like calculus and Maxwell's Equation. They require extra insight.

But look at Schrodinger. The H with the raised bar means total entropy. Heisenberg can be understood as energy cancellations. The small h with the cross means energy moment. The rest says that the observable energy at-moment equals the total observable entropy! Do you see what it is? It's how fusion reacts! It's the behavior of pure nuclear energy! (The double integral means the energy is conserved relative to energy).

Lorentz transformation is a version of velocity in which free-fall velocity and the speed of light are inversely related because of the effect of mass upon gravity.

Look at information theory. The H means tendency to equilibrium. Negative sum probability of x log probability of x means that the sum of scatter plot points, whether they are aligned or unaligned, tends to express as an S-curve related to the degree of equilibrium.

Chaos theory. Chaos theory is perhaps the simplest. It simply means change occurs relative to time and the existing condition of the system. In other words, large changes can occur over time, especially if something is highly complex, highly unusual things can occur.

Lagrangian: Is the property of modifying blobs by sphere-like impressions: generally it is as up as down, except that it tends to go down, depending on the ratio between the impression or extrusion and the mass of the blob, e.g. the sides of the extrusion tend to go down with wide intrusions in a large blob, ignoring physics.

Markov chains are cospookyons between past and future datapoints correlated to a particular place in a time sequence (for example using predictive modeling formulas). The synchronization of time and model-behavior allows greater data coherence than otherwise possible.

Cauchy sequence is the rule that a convergent sequence diminishes at a rate of x/y or y/x compared to the distance of the line relative to data equilibrium.

Bohmian Mechanics: spooky Platonic wave chaotic. + neuroscience $\rightarrow$ physics.

4-D flames look like a Klein Bottle elevation map.

Hydrodynamics: Gravity, flow, volume, viscosity, absorption: absorption is a property of the materials the fluid interacts with. Remember waves are caused by the moon.

Pauli Exclusion Principle: What keeps

quantum events separate, into separate paths of energy, for example, in a grid or tessellation with exceptionality (my terminology).

Other topics:

Cubic wave functions.

EXPLORING PHYSICS

I will describe the standard model of physics— Its really neat and compact.

There are six classifications of fermions, which happen to be divided into three classes or columns: Type I, Type II, and Type III.

I will list the particles in each row.

The first half is quarks, the second half is leptons.

All fermions have a spin of 1/2.

Up, Charm, and Top quarks have a charge of 2/3.

Down, Strange, and Bottom quarks have a charge of -1/3.

Now we begin the leptons.

Electrons, muons, and tau particles (which are leptons) have a charge of -1.

Electron neutrinos, muon neutrinos, and tau neutrinos have a charge of zero.

Now we pass on to the category called the gauge bosons. This only contains four classifications, so I will just read them.

All of these have a spin of 1, which is larger than 1/2.

Photons, gluons, Z bosons, and W bosons.

As an added detail, all of these have a charge of zero except the W boson, which is +/- 1.

(Listed from top to bottom next to the fermions).

Finally, we get to the scalar boson, and there is only one in this category, the Higgs boson, which has no charge and no spin.

There are also some additional facts about mass that are a little harder to remember, but at least you know that as far as this diagram of the Standard Model, all that is left is mass.

Now, think about this a minute.

All these particles, well most of them, are charges swirling, reacting, and sometimes reacting, sometimes annihilating. You might know about this if you are familiar with schrodinger's equation.

How do we know what they are all doing? Well, we have to know everything about them. But it turns out, according to quantum mechanics, we can't know!

We're half-blind, as it were, when it comes to the smallest particles. We can see the big, macro-world effects, but when it comes to the littlest, tiniest particles, it breaks down into indeterminate probability.

And here is the thing—we know only it's wave equation or its particle location, not

both—never both, unless someone deter-
mines —or finds—a new physics.

Very Platonic!

Not at all like biology!

Its like its in my head! That's what people
say when they have it memorized!

Also:

"Virtual photons carry electromagnetic
force, gluons carry the strong force, and
the Z and W bosons together carry the
weak force." —Matthew Pharr

HOW TO BE SMART #5
HOW TO BE A PROFESSOR

SCHOOL OF THE GIFTED

An impromptu writing summarizing the best insights on "teaching giftedness", if such is possible.

My mind is locked on log-i-cum—

I think a thought of something that thinks—

We comprehend what we believe—

A system is formed of just beliefs—

Beliefs that are formed are justly true—

What is false is neither, nor—

Death does not occur to original minds—

The greatest thought is a tempting nought—

What escapes a door?—

The true is esplendant, crystal minds!—

Who would pont a cure?—

The razor is the world in tines—

The miracle is demure!—

The fortune is cast in stone—

The reason is Latin—

The ruin is not sums—

The blade is truth—

The words are lost & found—

HOW TO BE A PROFESSOR PART 1

Cleavage and information theory.

Are you masturbating? (Psychologist getting on coat) thought of "you're thinking nothing, well I'm not either" and God is thinking.

Sorry, I wasn't thinking.

Where is the red marker when I need it?

Ively boobly baby.

This is going to be dirty.

Sorry professor, are you covering up
something?

Only words can tell.

What's wrong with the usual approach?

I'm an absent-minded professor.

What happens when we're down in the
slump?

We go diving for seagulls!

What's wrong with you today professor?

I've bit off more than I can chew. I feel like
I've bit the big one!

What's your answer?

I'm trying to put it together.

We're sorry for you, professor.

Nathan Coppedge

Oh, it's just me and my messy office.

We want to break a donut with you, prof.

It isn't my kind of day.

Pictures tell a thousand words, professor.

That picture's always been on my wall.

Why are you so grumpy, professor?

I don't know how to fight it. A field
change has come over the campus and I'm
too old to tolerate it. It's time to move on.

What aroused you so late at night?

The pickles are pickling.

I don't have words for you!

Menarche e los loanos.

Frequent flyer miles?

I want a different steward.

What's up?

Something's burning.

I'm going to break your nose.

Then we're not going to break even.

It's tempting isn't it, watching a young
girl, scantily clad, pose for pictures with
an unknown stranger, barely guessing his
name, and arousing an enticing entou-
rage?

You couldn't guess her name, either!

What are you looking at?

I think I just wrote one to Francisco
Jimenez (I think I just invented perpetual
motion).

Note: The above is "How To Be A Professor Part One".

HOW TO BE A PROFESSOR PART 2: SPE-CIALIZED LANGUAGE

Dock crumbs: misplaced oddities.

Saw through the epiphany: completely stupid.

Ideal diect: the law of the individual scholar.

Promisees: fateful discord.

Jundiced: temporarily immortal.

Proloquay: words of the bitterly departed.

Insequious: dawning.

Aprobe: big statement.

Horrussurus: something that sounds em-barrassing, but really isn't.

Pill: a common necessity.

HOW TO BE A PROFESSOR PART 3

Additional Complexity.

If you are Athena (discerning) and you
think of complexity (category), you should
think this is a grieve (sink), so it should
not hurt.

Let me explain this. I was thinking of extending my legs in bed, and they seemed
to extend over the lip (of land) and so
there was a sink (of land), that my legs
needed protection (grieves), so they
should not hurt, and so it might be called
complex, and I needed the discernment,
like Athena.

HOW TO BE SMART #6

REALIZING ONE'S ULTIMATE POR-POISE

"Being is the nearest. Yet the near remains farthest from man."

—Heidegger

(HEIDEGGER, M. Basic Writings. "Letter on Humanism". David Krell, Ed. p. 234).

Read the following techniques until you come to the conclusion. It will help you realize your brain:

Nathan's Immortality Techniques, Set #1:

(1) Make little bets with yourself about what something means. It could be whether you look at a car passing, or whether you choose to smile or eat a snack at a given moment. If it turns out one way, you decide that it has a given result. So you use it to hone your willpower. Not only that, but you use it to gain motivation about what you can really achieve. You can tell yourself, 'my smile means immor-

tality' or 'when I eat this snack, it's for a good reason, so I'm going to make some achievement'. Instead of being completely flexible, apply principle now and then, and use it as guidance for the long-term.

(2) See your own past as something that was infinitely old, and your future as something moderately young. This will allow you to justify endless good health. Life is not a sacrifice or something idiotic, but rather an endless struggle to regain lost wisdom, by becoming young. Youth will provide a platform for the infinite quest that is required.

(3) By your own definition, try to be lucid about your entire life whenever possible. This involves seeing through the mists of time that enshroud your life, and making some predictions about what will happen to you, and what your life means. This will make you relatively wise compared to people who do not do this.

(4) Do small things to improve your health incrementally as time goes on. By this logic, if you are infinitely old, you will definitely be infinitely healthy! Use this logic to convince yourself that you will

never die, or at least, when your health leaves, it was a robber who took it, not someone giving charity.

Nathan's Immortality Techniques, Set #2:

(1) Don't Make Evil Bargains. Obey your best principle. Your soul or sense of self-motivation is the deepest underlying principle related to you and your life.

(2) Practice Virtuous Health. Health is the best kind of karma, because you get the reward immediately. I am a deep believer that when you are healthy, others are healthy too. Don't believe appearances about others' sickness or sense of well-being. Trust improvement in your own life, and only when it improves!

(3) Have Principle. Creating laws to live by --- that you really believe in --- can make a difference for your perception of time and the prospect of immortality.

(4) Mix Ingredients in Your Mind. Practicing a little mental chemistry can make a huge difference in the long-term. Remember, its not about drugs, but your own sense of self. Even if you don't notice re-

sults from your thought process immediately, remember that where you have a principle, you can improve eventually! Where you have headaches, you may later have happiness! Where you have blunt emotions, you may later become vibrant! Miracles are possible with a good brain!

Nathan's Immortality Techniques, Set #3:

(1) Permutations of interpretation. Infinite dimensions of time, forgettable, exposable.

(2) Periods of activity and inactivity.

(3) Ironic about the negative. An attitude of delayed indifference.

(4) Ask originality of objects, leave it ambiguous if they do not reply.

Nathan's Immortality Techniques Set #4:

(1) Ritual.

(2) Distraction.

(3) Patience.

(4) Permanentize.

Nathan's Immortality Techniques, Set #5:

(1) Peace.

(2) Metabolic metaphysics.

(3) Avoid poisonous feelings.

(4) Phenomenally ascend / transcend. E.g. like having lucid thoughts about Platonism or transcendental phenomenology.

In this case, unlike most cases of transcendence, the emphasis is on the metaphysics.

Nathan's Immortality Techniques, Set #6:

(1) The original re-collection as one's 'momentary consciousness'.

(2) If two things are equal, consider that the alternative may be just as good.

(3) Learn from alien life, like chickens and metiorites.

(4) Know when sacred space is sacred, and when it is cursed. Life depends on it.

Nathan's Immortality Techniques, Set #7:

(1) Choose something good for your brain. Meaningful substance.

(2) Have a method. For example, how to feel immortal when you feel like it. How to be ambitious like an immortal.

(3) Improve on the method. For example, how to feel immortal more easily. How to know medicine and feel healthy at will.

(4) Practice grace of form and function. The true moral. This involves finding the grace of God.

(5) Know everyone has their own kind of meaning. The seperation of the bodies (into different immortals). The living will, the ultimate purpose, the gift of identity, etc.

Conclusion:

One's immediately prior life was effec-tively an 'ultimate porpoise (dolphin)'.

One's (anyone's) life before that if they had three lives so far was as 'the Living Will' a kind of stupid religious figure.

It turns out, remembering the dolphin is exactly how to have a brain. When in doubt, think of your basal ganglia.

Then you may consider Techniques #9, where it is said:

1. The attitude of something-better-than-righteousness.

2. A vision-of-the-world.

3. True-thought-dwelling-within-the-vision.

4. The self-emerging from the thought.

Truly a key to true thought!

HOW TO BE SMART #7

THE PHILOSOPHY OF EDMUND HUSSERL

In retrospect… 'My mind exploded'… What everyone says…

I have read parts of his confusingly-named Cartesian Meditations and other works in translation, and I was at first both impressed and not impressed.

I have taken the trouble to reread it with guidance from a seminar I once attended, and I now think it is worth reading, although far more difficult to understand than works written in plain English.

Here is an overview of the deep side of Husserl's Meditations for the record, but sometimes its much more fun to read the book, if only because Husserl sounds like a heroin addict (hard to explain):

'SIMPLE' OVERVIEW OF HUSSERL'S CARTESIAN MEDITATIONS:

I.

Absolutes are radical. Think like a Cubist
with two imaginary berets on your head.
Have a soul or make art.
7. Nature, nature, nature, nature, even so,
we are the only evidence of nature.

8. Being is only being qua being.

11. Victimization.

II.

12. Orthology our hero. Post-modern land-
scape is potentially unreal.

13. Should God take drugs. Give him a
break… negative paradox.

15. The ego surrounds the self perceptibly
to itself. We are what we feel, and we are
rational afterwards.

17. The subjective can objectify.

18. The peculiarity of the ordinary. Singu-
lar medium of organic respiration. Watch
out!

19. Alien phenomenology: so-called

'whorable events'. Noesis e o noesos.

20. Awareness processes.

III.

25. Serious play.

27. Creative destruction.

IV.

30. The phenomena moves through you.

32. I am as I believe—Aha!

HOW TO BE SMART #8

ARCHETYPE STUDIES

1.

PHILOSOPHY AS FERMAT

"The aesthetic of Fermat is said to be sche-
mat."

—Unknown

Basically, there is an ideal concept of many
things.

The ideal concept can be ideally represented.

Ideally, it has ideal functions, which I take
to mean simple logic functions with profound consequences.

In some cases, this logic function can be
represented by the ideal visual.

In other cases, more complex visuals or
combinatorial organizations of visuals
may be required to create ideal logic, and

thus the ideal concepts.

If the logic is imperfect, it is abandoned without additional analysis.

Thus we get potentially many seperate systems, each operating under its own formalism.

Assuming all structures are symbolic, they can be integrated through common logic functions. This may result in abbreviation, categorization, or preference of one system over another.

It becomes clear that some systems are preferable for some specific purposes. I have done a lot of the work. There may be some overlap.

Visual methods become the index of formal tools. However, they are inflected by assumptions about the meaning of formalism.

Suddenly, the figure-ground is concerned primarily, first-most, with meta-critique.

Thus, we take ' the Meta' as it is called, which is an abstraction for this process, and, through the imposition of many arbitrary tools upon this object, we reach the formal aesthetics of logic.

That is how we do Fermat.

Basically the implication is there are many functional objects, and some functions are totals.

The Format Critique of Fermat:

That science doesn't have a format.

2.

OBJECTIVE ALCHEMY

One property may become another when taken to an extreme.

Extreme properties can be cancelled because of laws about general physical behavior.

One qualification lemma can lead to the multiple-representation of properties.

Thus, materials are really principles of the

realization of properties.

The second lemma is that physics can be further conditioned by exceptional cases (technology, improbability, perceptibility, magic) to realize any property once the material is flexible, and once the principle of realization has been realized.

See also: Alchemy

3.

COHERENT SILLHOUETTES

There are different modes, which get different results.

There are various scales. Vast differences. Great distances.

Something may be seen in sillhouettte. With high contrast. Something may matter more than another, like religion or science or the planet Earth.

Depending on all this, there are particular ways of viewing and understanding the silhouette, which are also important, and which are the schemas of any particular viewpoint, however obscure. And these things may be the thoughts associated with realizing what is highly contrasting which is also what is most real.

4.

WILBER'S INTEGRALISM

Wave Functions

That mathematical knowledge is about waves. That these waves permeate being.

Integrity

That everything that is, has integrity. We should find confirmation for all that truly is. What must be has the virtue of spirit.

Core Essentialism

Realizing that basically one is a baby.

Social Reality

That one should communicate the essentials of one's purpose. That one should think of the whole equation.

Dharma

That genius is the existence. That not all existence is perfect. That perfection must be appreciated.

Action

That the science of behavior has a principle of intelligence. That actions must judge their distance carefully.

The Wheel

That there is a common wheel or web which binds people, and is like a brain. That God is much like society.

Work

That there is no problem which cannot be solved. That problems may require time, money, and work to solve.

5.

PREMIER PSYCHOLOGY

How to break down the barrier of madness?

By admitting very early there is a wall. For
example, if arbitrary seems crazy and
crazy is assumed to be schizophrenic or
depressive or scary, then it is time to break
down the wall of the arbitrary very early.
It is often a rewarding experience.

The very existence of symbolic behaviors
is often enough to create the sanity within
the mind, ultimately, if the behaviors are
symbolic enough.

In this way, as Jung cited, the rationality is
the utilization of symbols.

In the desperate cases, the answer is to be
concerned with what concerns others, because it is this quality which has been so
successful at locking the extrovert within
the social caccoon.

The discovery of harmony after wave
functions is very often only slightly less
advanced than this knowledge of the social caccoon.

And as knowledge, it is experience, something extroverts know very well.

6.

THE LIVING TRUTH

If someone says you are being too ambiguous, you can say…

Everyone wants to be the living truth.

Existence is composed entirely of good and bad ideas of women.

Maybe the living truth is PART of a woman, or part of a man…

7.

TALK

Fairness is impossible because of virtue.

You see, everyone is different.

The soul is not always composed.

And not every composition has a soul.

But they are at war.

8.

WORLD & UNIVERSE

In Platonism, the universe is where the worlds collide, and that is when they become universal.

9.

Mad men may be great or good.

10.

The word 'evil' is likely to cause evil, except for perverts.

11.

Sometimes thought is just a principle. This bears repeating.

…

HOW TO BE SMART #9

THE GREAT UNDERSTANDING PART 1: THE MAGICALLY-MISCELLANEOUS STUDY AID

Also called "The Great Understanding Part 1".

A point

Quality A domain A (hard beginning point)

A&A&A (unimportant company)

AAAA (unimportant company for unimportant people, or just scream)

B production

Quality B domain B (business as usual)

B&B&B (lots of music)

BBBB (center of attention)

C sector (not 'section')

Quality C domain C (ordinary hero)

C&C&C (hardly needed)

Product CCCC (against wall)

D fancy

Quality D domain D (not fancy)

D&D&D (high quality last-minute)

DDDD (superficial land)

E compass

Quality E domain E (lost exploring)

E&E&E (found something)

What you need EEEE (extra efficient energy engine, four types of equipment, effectively evading everyone entirely)

F do

Quality F domain F (something unpredictable)

F&F&F (angry: form, function, and futil-
ity)

Loud noise FFFF (deflation)

G pass

Quality G domain G (I predict more 'G')

G&G&G (it was probably a joke)

Art GGGG (fancy cover-up)

H item

Quality H domain H (two properties)

H&H&H (boring, don't try it)

HHHH (excitement)

I omega

Quality I domain I (something personal)

I&I&I (straight woman)

Incorrect IIII (IV)

J misfire

Quality J domain J (something casual about J)

J&J&J ('never' actually happens)

Liberal JJJJ (almost never happens)

K measure

Quality K domain K (calculus)

K&K&K (scarily outside domain)

Crap KKKK (really bad sign)

L factor (infinity)

Quality L domain L (obvious)

L&L&L (something long and intimidating)

Go LLLL (sports)

M theory

Quality M Domain M (magical metaphysics)

M & M & M (Motley)

Magical MMMM (mandate manifesto of multifarious meaning)

N notation

Quality N Domain N (neural network)

N & N & N (neuro-opsing, neuro-computing, and neuro-imaging)

Network NNNN (No-nonsense neural network)

O truth

Quality O domain O (orthographic ordering)

O&O&O (Order counts, order matters, order disappears)

Ontology OOOO (objectively ordered orthographic ontology)

P parsing

Quality P domain P (pure potential)

P&P&P (pure, potent, perfect)

Program PPPP (pre-programmed perfect potential)

Q gate

Quality Q domain Q (qualified quantity)

Q&Q&Q (quit, quote, and quiet: advice)

Quality QQQQ (just means queue the quality)

R state

Quality R domain R (statement about R)

R&R&R (sometimes we overdo it)

Real RRRR (real risk realer relevence: principle of metaphysics)

S type

Quality S domain S (stipulation about S)

S&S&S (senses, sensoriums, and sciences: are advanced)

Science SSSS (Super-solving science system: generic solution to everything)

T theory

Quality T domain T (truth-theoretic, take it from there)

T&T&T (take-in, tool-out, and turn-over: processing)

Token TTTT (for example there's that truth thing)

U label

Quality U domain U (underwater →floats up / unitarian → universalist)

U&U&U (when you're going up you must be going up. Up, up: up, but what does up mean?)

Universal UUUU (Silence: utterance under ubiquitous untruths)

V science (piloting)

Quality V domain V (vision and vertigo: flight)

V&V&V (view, verify, and vantage: aerial combat)

Vortex VVVV (very vivid vortex in view)

W plan

Quality W domain W (a world for workers, wide world)

W&W&W (weak, weaker, and washed-out: contingency)

Wizard WWWW (world wishes with the world)

X line

X quality X domain (hearing yes or no?)

X&X&X (stupidity… complain)

Perfect XXXX (something powerful)

Y design

Quality Y domain Y (something fashionable)

Y&Y&Y (conditioning)

Year YYYY (0000 - 9999)

Z compromise

Quality Z domain Z (something new)

Z&Z&Z (prophets)

Angle ZZZZ (don't lose your leg!)

…

THE GREAT UNDERSTANDING PART 2

1. Find your most obvious key attribute. For example, big ears, a big nose, or liking to do taxes.

2. (Repeat as necessary).

3. If you are flawed, what is it that makes this attribute flawed?

4. If you are perfect, what is it that makes this attribute perfect?

5. What in your life does this symbol (the attribute) represent?

6. What might your strategy be?

You may find that this is the type of question that defines your life, and it matters very much how optimistic you are.

(I, for one, have big ears I'm serious. My response was to try to be a foolish genius).

THE GREAT UNDERSTANDING PART 3

1. Receiving gifted treatment.

2. Knowing how to be a professor.

3. Conversant in the language.

4. Having a ready tongue.

5. Being outspoken.

6. Performing tactfully.

7. Using language games.

8. Making use of reserves of knowledge.

9. Studying examples.

10. Making use of illustrations.

11. (Sane explorations).

HOW TO BE SMART #10

INTELLIGENT REMARKS

Just point at it, that grants it a matter-of-fact.

One might try to recollect one's recollection.

A Chinese god invented double-oppositeness, in the end poisoning his friend.

Inane atttaction to other species' feces.

The postmodern urge to do the ridiculous.

The metamodern urge to drop the 'ism'.

The dimensional handicap of viewing each thing only as its quality.

HOW TO BE SMART #11

PREMIER PSYCHOLOGY

PREMIER PSYCHOLOGY 1

Sane Mind / Enlightened Thinking

You approach the day with a clear mind.

You go to an art gallery, where the to-and-fro movement of people reminds you of the blossoming of a rose.

Then the rose withers, and it is replaced with a lotus.

Deep within the walls of the building, you have the same old thought you had when you were a child, that the only way out is generosity.

How to break down the barrier of madness?

By admitting very early there is a wall. For example, if arbitrary seems crazy and crazy is assumed to be schizophrenic or depressive or scary, then it is time to break down the wall of the arbitrary very early. It is often a rewarding experience.

The very existence of symbolic behaviors is often enough to create the sanity within the mind, ultimately, if the behaviors are symbolic enough.

In this way, as Jung cited, the rationality is the utilization of symbols.

In the desperate cases, the answer is to be concerned with what concerns others, because it is this quality which has been so successful at locking the extrovert within the social caccoon.

The discovery of harmony after wave functions is very often only slightly less advanced than this knowledge of the social caccoon.

And as knowledge, it is experience, something extroverts know very well.

PREMIER PSYCHOLOGY 2

Identity problem. Identify a problem.

General problem. Specific function.

Functional paradigm. Minimal suffering.

Luxury platform. Philosophical paradise.

PREMIER PSYCHOLOGY 3

Now we will address your morality.

Here is what I want to say:

"There is no need to believe in white lies, there is no need to believe in dark truths. It was a dream."

What do you think? You probably think you feel too impure to come to terms with this new eidõs.

But guess what? If you felt good, you would be naive, which is just as bad. One way or another you need to experience life.

Now you feel an angel on one shoulder
and an imp on the other. That's how it
should be!

It turns out, if its not a dream, we
SHOULD believe in those things: we
should BELIEVE in the white lies and dark
truths! Can you stand it?

But let's take it back. Let's say you were
perfect and pure. You wouldn't have any
need to believe in either of them, hypo-
thetically.

You see, either you're good, or your vision
is clouded.

What about the dream? Well, the dream is
neither good nor evil, it is both. The moment we believe it is evil or good is the
moment we're talking to the angel and the
imp.

Are they more real? Well, they are just a
metaphor, it is a psychological process that
plays out.

PREMIER PSYCHOLOGY 4

What's the completion of psychology?
Atheism.

Atheism is the doctrine that things are as
they appear.

Without exaggeration, you can't believe in
anything.

There is no room for superstitious mythol-
ogy.

Sensations are just as they are, no exaggeration.

You know what atheism is? Sanity.

Atheism is the way to reject ridiculous beliefs without making a ridiculous statement.

Now, if you do calculus, its advanced.

Now, if you have beliefs, it means something.

Because now you actually care.

That's atheism.

Clean, pure true atheism.

And we must be atheists, because beliefs lead us astray. We know that from our moral lesson.

PREMIER PSYCHOLOGY 5

When you're done with what you're do-ing, you'll put on your ecclesiastical cape and rid the world of hunger.

No, why not?

Because you said 'no'.

Oh, that's a profound answer. But, really you wouldn't you see, no one would. Hu-mans are evil. But that doesn't make good not worth trying.

No, you're evil. You're an evil therapist.

Oh, that's an important discovery, psycho-logically. But I'm not evil, you see. I'm teaching you about morality.

I don't see the point, if you are convinced the world is evil and therefore pointless and therefore worthless.

That's not the point at all. The point is really a noble one and a good one, but no one human is fully capable, that is what I am saying.

But, I am fully capable.

(There, you got something!)

PREMIER PSYCHOLOGY 6

I once knew a valedictorian who did not get colds. She said whenever she was about to get a cold, she rubbed water on her nose and it went away.

This speaks of a certain different attitude among the mental elite.

My Dad for one once remarked that he thought something was up with me.

Is there something wrong with what you

say to yourself when you breathe? He
said?

I think my breaths are saying 'seig heil' I
said.

I thought as much! He said. Why don't
you try saying something nicer, like: 'I
think now I feel healthy'? That way you'll
take bigger breaths and you won't feel so
scared of people, and you'll have a reason
to feel probably much better!

But, I said, I'm worried I'll feel depressed
and weird, because 'seig heil' is what I
think breaths sound like, and reassuring
myself all the time sounds depressing!

I know, he said, but I know you'll feel better. Psychologists can say whatever they
want, but it is how you feel that matters.

So I tried it later when I was alone and
what came out was 'he feels fine' — and I
did feel better about people, and life got
better.

Note: I am not a Nazi, so of course 'seig
heil' was just my paranoia manifesting un-
controllably.

HOW TO BE SMART #12
GIFTED POEMS

PEDDLEBERY POEM

(With hints from my brother Brian the prodigy, who may have wrote a similar poem years ago…).

Merry, merry peddlebery sits in a tree!

Merry peddlebery is as gifted as can be!

Peddlebery, what does he think of the tree?

Peddlebery, what if he is knocked from the tree?

What do we say of peddlebery's tree?

What do we say of the image of a tree?

Peddlebery sits and thinks its a tree?

Then how can he not fall from out of the tree?

We know we're right when we say peddlebery and rhyme with a tree!

Unfortunately the only way to rhyme is to use the word 'tree'!

When we use the word 'tree' we want to knock him out of the tree!

But without peddlebery it wouldn't be a tree!

Note: this was actually written after I read the Birth of Tragedy, but is listed earlier in How to Be Smart.

THE LUCID ELYSIUM

High-minded thoughts without dystopia.

Teenagers masturbate without dystopia.

Impregnate clouds and think about them.

The world is somewhat right of the Utopia.

What rare tools will make us win?

The Lucid Elysium.

HOW TO BE SMART #13

FREUD, DEATH, AND THE BIRTH OF TRAGEDY

—A paper that is really about Nietzsche, not Freud. —

Nietzsche draws an early distinction between dreams as statues and music as intoxication (33). That is his departure point, which I would like to connect with Nietzche's oft-declared love of Plato as well as, in this case, Dionysus. Nietzsche makes use of the theme of Apollo and Dionysus in a conspicuous way when the text is analyzed. But it is also important to connect the apparent analytic theme of the work with the apparent, although also subtle expressed theme, which it turns out is different— the theme of death. Before we realize a Freudian motive here on Nietzsche's part, it would be better to realize his intentions in communicating the theme of tragedy. So, first I will explain Nietzsche's theme of tragedy, and then I will extirpate the more hidden analytic theme underlying the Apollo and Dionysus— for that is indeed the metaphysical theme of this work, in effect the miraculous mirror image of Thus Spake Zarathustra. Here Nietzsche sews his myth of eternal beginning, his tragedy about Apollo, a claim I cannot prove, but which, at least so far as the mirror image, supports the idea that Nietzsche has something divine in mind.

The author soon begins to write terrifyingly suggesting that Dionysus is a mere image of Apollo: "All forms speak to us, there is nothing unimportant or superfluous… mere appearance. [Italics his]." (34) When Nietzsche mentions Schopenhauer's dream images he appears to be equating death with classicism itself, a figure almost as radical as equating Apollo with Dionysus, and it appears to be an extension of this. When we compare Nietzsche's statement of the "divine comedy of life [itself]" (35) we get the helpful image of the statue of the god Zeus— which suggests that if Apollo and Dionysus are going to be united, and we favor Apollo, and Apollo is the soul of images— then the soul itself is a kind of summation, and so the Statue of all statues becomes the Summa Imaga, connected in a later reference to Maya (illusion) and so to the analytic theme of Plato and Socrates.

Nietzsche is beginning to analyze death by considering it as a statue, for that is what a doctor would observe about a dead body.# For Nietzsche, the Apollonian dream world (for Apollo was god of dreams) speaks of the idea that the Dionysian is a lie, but that this means the soul is not dead. However, he also alludes to the idea that the soul is Apollo, and that Apollo, as master of illusion, is also master of the underworld. And this becomes obvious with the comparison of the 'underworld' and 'dream world', which might easily mean the same thing, if the truth indeed consists of statues.

Nietzsche also alludes (35) to the idea that the work of the ambiguously Dionysian muses is in fact in some way the death of the soul, the sacrifice of the true soul for the soul-image#: "[Our] innermost being... experiences dreams with profound delight and joyous necessity. [Italics mine]." In other words, he is equating pleasure with death. This is the beginning of the idea that Nietzsche is in touch with something Freudian. But it is more important to realize that he is developing the theme of what death symbolizes, a theme that will later translate into other more modern ones.#

It is worth noting that we could criticize Nietzsche with the idea that he believes too strongly in the Greek triumphant hero— whether of tragedy, or comedy, god or mortal. But what Nietzsche has to say is far too important to be interrupted. There is a growing hint, however, of other gods than the ones he mentioned— for example, if Apollo is dead, since life comes from the false image, then we could think that cruelly-depicted Minerva was behind the false image, and that in effect philosophy was at the root of this ugliness. "Even when [the eye of Apollo] …. is angry and distempered it is still hallowed by beautiful illusion"!

Nietzsche is now willing to compare BOTH Dionysus and Apollo with the image of the frail Christian motif Everyman, but since Nietzsche is talking about psychological individuation, what he means is that the Matrix is the soul. This is yet another progression of his concept of death, specifically an image of postmodern dystopianism, and he goes on to helpfully illustrate with the idea that pleasure is a problem. He says that pleasure allows "a glimpse into the nature of the Diony-sian" (36) which he has just declared to be an oxymoron.

However, not all is lost to the gods, for they have a terrible secret, which he describes in Midas' (mortal) encounter with the immortal Silenus#. Silenus says:

"Oh, wretched ephemeral race, children of chance and misery… What is best of all is utterly beyond your reach: not to be born, not to be, to be nothing."

Thus, Nietzsche is driving home the idea that gods are just as miserable as men, and so there is at last no defense for Everyman, in spite of his Dante-esque condition. And Nietzsche alludes to how this means Oresteia is an 'un-bearable' play.

You will excuse me if I continue to follow the text in a linear fashion. The themes of dreams as intoxication and devil as death now come together: "[The] truly existent primal unity, eternally suffering and con-tradictory, also needs the rapturous vision, the pleasurable illusion, for its continuous redemption. [Italics mine]." (45). The key now is that the dream itself is a sacrifice, and so he suggests that there is a choice between a soul and a lie, one the soul being unconscious, and the lie being pleasure at great cost. Now Nietzsche writes "[This apotheosis]… the delimiting of the boundaries of the individual [are] measure in a Hellenic sense." (46). What he means by a measure of apotheosis in a Hellenic sense could only mean individual-as-sacrifice, another yet more audacious depiction of the Freudian Id (death). This is easily reflected in the importance of Greek theatre for the Greeks, and the importance of the Greek gods for Greek theatre. For what is more important to the Greeks than either the separation of Dionysus or the great sacrifice of the gods that permits them to be born from him? And yet, that is a depiction of Greek theatre! At this point our author begins to be involved in a very dark eidõs.

Now let us clarify Nietzsche's core psychological conflict — if there is one — in light of Nietzsche's relation to another figure Wagner, who although I know that he was a German composer in a sense represents to Nietzsche the future of Greek theatre as well as the impulse of the muses, which Nietzsche increasingly thinks is Apollonian rather than Dionysian, (since Apollo represents the hidden 'inner image' in other words, Socrates). Wagner also represents Nietzsche's love of German folk culture, including the pastoral and artistic images which originally owe their existence to Greece. As I am unfamiliar with Wagner and much of his work is music, I will not touch on the exact specifics of why he appealed to Nietzsche. However, there is another theme which touches on Nietzsche's potential conflict, and that is his (Nietzsche's) personal lustfulness, which appears in one particular passage:

[Being] in longing of a Buddhistic negation of the will… a lethargic element… As soon as this everyday reality re-enters reality, it is experienced as [Dionysian]. (59)

We can now imagine a certain pastoral attachment to lust, representing women, but associated with Wagner the folk-hero. This is a critical element, as Nietzsche's views on death will not be authentically understood without an understanding of his meaning of the Id.

Nietzsche introduces a new concept, a kind of sine-wave death-ray, when he describes the dialectic between Dionysus and Apollo. He describes them both as 'inexorable' aspects of Greek culture:

And so, wherever the Dionysian prevailed the Apollinian was checked and destroyed [that is, Dionysius made huge waves]…on the other hand, it is equally certain that, wherever the … [Dionysian was] successfully withstood, the authority and majesty of [Apollo] exhibited itself as more rigid and menacing than ever [in other words, Apollo always had the middle ground, if not the high ground].

(47)

He has already described both as representing death, first-most through the image of Silenus (or Sardonicus), and second-most through the comparison of death with dreams. Now he is presenting another outrageous image, of two deaths doing a kind of battle. Now Nietzsche alludes to the "titanic-barbaric nature of the Dionysian" immediately after mentioning the 'Doric' (still known today for Doric architecture, which is not just columns but a sine-wave like entablature motif) and the earlier mention of a sort of sine-wave death ray now gives us the suggestion that the Dionysian's last defense is to 'drop the ceiling' on the Apollonians. This is in fact an obscure reference to how both gods could be destroyed by anathema, for after all, anything can be destroyed by anathema, and anathema might represent Athena, which in turn expresses one of the dangling themes about philosophy as the nature of the hidden image.

All of this is important to understand Nietzsche's following symbol of a "child, at once Antigone and Cassandra," (47) which it turns out is the beginning of his references to the division of the body of Dionysus, which is one of his most important images. It is later clarified that the division of the body of Dionysus is an image of Greek culture: "ragged tatters of ancient tradition have been sewn together in various combinations and torn apart again."(56) But I will focus less on the division than I will on its importance as a symbol for philosophy. Certainly it does support the Apollonian argument for modern theatre through the later importance of the body of Dionysus for Socrates, but that is one of the more complex themes, and I do not have time to discuss it. However, what can be shown on the simplest level is that Antigone represents human strife, while Cassandra represents divine strife (Moira) #, and thus, the image of the child clearly represents Socrates, reinforced by the earlier conclusion that philosophy is the precious weapon anathema. As far as Socrates and the collapsing Greek temple, the conclusion is that the weakness of philosophy turns out to be the death of theatre.

However, Nietzsche soon turns this image on its head, first with a battle of the humors: "The first 'objective' artist confronts the first 'subjective' artist" (48) (referring to Homer and Archilochus). Nietzsche says that Apollo is the law, and Dionysus is usually naïve. Modern lyric poetry, which I can now identify as a symbol for Socrates, is called "a statue of a god without a head" (49) completing the motif of the statue-as-dead-person. Now the statue has become death personified. At this point it has reached a crazy height where any sort of symbol could have irony, which is one of Nietzsche's important points about modernism. Humor is the development of the Sardonicus just as Socrates develops from the Dionysian, but all it does is add to the terrible irony.

Now when Nietzsche talks of 'primal unity' it is clear he is referring to a death image. And so, when he says music is a representation of primal unity, he is really saying that music is a representation of death, or at least an image of a representation. However, he also says that the divine artist is not naïve. He describes the transcendence of Archilochus into godhood in just such a way (50). For Nietzsche, this ascendence is both ironic and inevitable, as the poet could be just an image.

"Does he know anything of the eternal essence of art; for in this state he is, in a marvelous manner like the weird image… which can turn its eyes at will and behold itself…" (52) "…hence language as the organ and symbol of phenomena, can never by any means disclose the innermost heart of music." (55) "Hellene … comforts [herself]" (59) "Not reflection, no—true knowledge, an insight into the horrible truth, outweighs any motive for action, both in Hamlet and in the Dionysian man." (60) "And as a satyr, in turn, he sees

the god." (64) True dreamers are Dionysian and see the tragedy of Apollo. "…the
womb that gave birth to the whole of the
so-called dialogue, that is, the entire
world…" (65)

References

NIETZSCHE, F. The Birth of Tragedy and
The Case of Wagner. Walter Kaufmann,
trans. NY: Vintage, 1967.

HOW TO BE SMART #14
ENLIGHTENED THINKING

ET1

THE CLASSIC OF IMMORTALITY

He must become great to prolong his life.

His greatness must be small, then he will have good health.

When the smallness is great, he presents an immortal face to the world.

Now, if he lives wisely and presents an immortal face, that is what is meant by immortality at first.

If he is always great, he will always present a wise face, and so it will be possible to overcome the most basic limitations.

If everything is understood, there is opportunity.

If there is a complete immortal opportunity, that may be sufficient for absolute greatness.

After that, we turn our minds to timeless thoughts.

ET2

THE GENIUS OF GREEK

Posted here as a reference.

Alpha waves: learn Calculus.

Beta: about business.

Gamma: choose a religion.

Delta: learn to use delta.

Eta: do things fast.

Zeta: learn about drugs.

Epsilon: control your urges.

Theta: gain knowledge.

Iota: demonstrate perfection.

Kappa: explore politics.

Lambda: ambitiously extend your activity.

Mu: learn how to die.

Nu: learn how to collect intelligence.

Omicron: learn advanced studies.

Pi: re-learn everything you've learned,
only better.

Rho: become a legend.

Sigma: become a doctor.

Tau: become unique.

Upsilon: rule the world.

Phi: teach.

Chi: make deals.

Psi: think.

Intermediate: applications.

Omega: pleasure, and politesse.

ET3

PEDDLEBERY POEM (SEE GIFTED PO-
EMS)

ET4

MITHRADOTALISM (SEE MEDICINE)

ET5

CHARACTERISTICS OF INFINITY

Related to the earlier writing originally de-
scribing the infinite goldfish: Wonders of
Dimensions

It's not a sandbox.
It's just a guppy.
The philosopher has quite an appetite.
Archetypes lock together.
Related to the later writing: Observations
on the Infinite Goldfish

And, Infinite Dimensional Heuristics

ET6

SANE MIND

You approach the day with a clear mind.

You go to an art gallery, where the to-and-fro movement of people reminds you of the blossoming of a rose.

Then the rose withers, and it is replaced with a lotus.

Deep within the walls of the building, you have the same old thought you had when you were a child, that the only way out is generosity.

ET7

PREMIER PSYCHOLOGY (SEE PREMIER PSYCHOLOGY)

ET8

PHILOSOPHY OF WORLD WAR II

I will focus on a particular moment in which saint devil whispered in someone's ear:

"Say: I'm the 108th airborne, and this is as far as those bastards are going."

Well, that's what he said, and the Germans eventually lost the war. But that attitude embodied by the 108th airborne was the subject of an entire ironic philosophy. You see, it was genius, genius out of place.

He (that character, part genius and part soldier) could just as easily have said in other circumstances:

I'm the 108th airborne, let's get this shit out of here!

I'm the 108th airborne, and my enemies are dead.

Knowledge is power, and I'm the 108th airborne

I'm the 108th airborne who knew war could be this easy?

War is a matter of faith, that's what makes me a civilian.

The attitude was not one of soldiers, but of dominant intelligence. The depth of the statement could make someone cry, even if they did not find the soldier attractive.

The genius behind it was the genius of God, or perhaps the genius of Saint Devil. Saint Devil knew the Germans would never win a war against a God with big ears. And on faith, it was nothing other than the wrath of God.

How is it brilliant to think big ears are un-interesting? Then how could it be worse than uninteresting? How is it brilliant to think anything is uninteresting? (But if God is not interested… everybody dies). That's what we mean by a God with big ears.

ET9

LA GRANDE JATTE

There is a memory I have of wandering periodically in Edgerton Park near the border of New Haven and Hamden on Whitney Ave.

On this particular time I imagined that all the other people I saw —It was summer, so it looked sort of like a Seurat painting — were epiphenomena, passing very quickly, yet leisurely, between neighborhoods of space, like actors in a movie set, perhaps tipping their hat, or time-traveling, etc so as to be on their way.

When I remember the scene I am reminded of a particular painting which is not by Seurat, but is very similar. Perhaps it is a photograph, or it is drawn painstakingly— It depicts a couple walking just at the edge of a fog near a forest. One gets an overwhelming sense of passing time, the urgency of the moment, like the fog represents time itself, following behind them.

When I think of this park I think of the

Seurat painting La Grande Jatte and this anonymous painting of the couple near the fog, and surprisingly I am reminded of the necessity of letting the world pass away. It reminds me that I can stay the same, even when worlds change.

It is this thought which most frequently marks me with wisdom. Simply the willingness to be wise, and yet remain unchanged by that.

ET10

THE METAMORPHOSIS*

(1)

Wouldn't that be nice? A new ornamental X, a new filligree Y…

It leads to ideas about life…

It might lead one to think great things…

It might lead one to lead a new life…

(2)
One has a certain degree of tolerance.
Then one notices…

There is an ancient problem. An archaic bug.

The bug, although it is old, has enmeshed itself in everything.

Now one requires a critical attitude. Everything outside the self is corrupt.

(3)

There is a remaining problem. One thing doesn't work.

One conducts some kind of process on the thing.

Some kind of energized occurrence happens. "Lightning comes down."

Suddenly you are trespassing on God.

*Originally written as The Errata of the Archana of History / The Intellectual Part 2

ET11

THE CONSTRUCTION OF THE SUBLIME SOUL

1.

It seems to me we should trust our close neighbors. They have knowledge of our materials. And if we are surrounded by aliens, then we should only trust parts of ourselves. And these parts of ourselves can be somewhat separate from who we really are if we do not realize ourselves.

Thus, if we do not realize ourselves, we can still trust part of ourselves which is a neighbor to ourselves, but which our not-so-neighborly neighbors do not consider part of ourselves. We can also transform into others like our neighbors, but only after incorporating parts of ourselves which are not yet parts of ourselves.

So, what is meant by neighbors is those closest to ourselves, even if it does not call itself our neighbor. For a lot of us are not officially neighbors to anyone, or not in the same capacity as those great beings which call themselves our neighbors, and family, and friends, and leaders, and so on.

Our neighbors may be great even though they do not call themselves great, because they are a different material from us. They are differentiated from our immediate process of constructing our soul. They have already realized something which we are not.

And yet it may not always be great to realize what we are not. At times, the best materials are not things that have been represented, but things which remain obscure, mysterious, magical, and abstract. But we should not destroy ourselves on the mere assumption that these magical things are more important than who we are.

2.

Ideas are the real things that we must realize when we encounter the otherness of the things within ourselves. The idea is neither separate nor precisely the same as us. It is, in its essence a composition with a purpose for the soul.

It is important not only to have ideas, but to differentiate between one idea and another, and purportedly to identify each idea with some aspect of our soul. But not all ideas are friendly neighbors. We may have selfish reasons to consider one idea most important, and another idea deservedly obscure.

It is only the best ideas which deserve to be part of the soul, but it is also true that not all souls are great enough to have a great many ideas. Nor is it deserving to be unrealistic if there is no real identification between the soul and its object.

Therefore, in this way, ideas are sometimes obscure, and they are sometimes idealizations. Simply because the soul does not rightfully identify with them unless it is very good. Yet there is no hard rule which makes the soul incapable of identifying with any of them.

As a rule, a soul can identify with some ideas, it is simply that in the worst case this identification is not very good. The lowly soul begins with a bad identification, gains a hazy idea, gains greater ideas, then becomes more ideal, and is able to identify with them.

Thus, intellectualization is a spiritual process, but it is more base than the fundamental ability of knowing neighbors. Knowing neighbors is the fundamental identification with ideas, while the actual realization of the soul is higher than that.

3.

Identification of the soul with ideas is fundamental, yet if the soul is already realized, it may be automatic. The natural soul realizes natural ideas, while the intellectual soul realizes intellectual ideas. The object of the soul is to become natural, yet the natural soul may not be intellectual.

There is nothing fundamental about ideas which makes the soul intellectual. Instead, the soul is superior to ideas. Understanding ideas creates the soul, yet the natural soul no longer requires ideas. The ideas of the higher soul are merely neighbors.

The ideas of the higher soul need not exist as ideas, but as real things. These things are as much neighbors as they are other people or parts of the soul. The soul exists in these things.

The purpose of the lower soul is to be realized, but this is no more than the relation
of neighbors, which is a bad identification,
a hazy idea, a collection of ideas, an identification, or the realization of the soul.

4.

Realizing the soul is a matter of sublime
existence. The simple manner of this existence is to have good emotion. Good emotion may require wisdom. Wisdom may
require the materials of sublime existence.

The way to acquire emotions is through
meaningful existence. Significance can create the materials which in turn create wisdom. When there is a fundamental way,
there can be a path to a sublime way.

What is more fundamental than meaning
or emotion is the sublime emotion, but this
only takes place in the sublime world.
Thus, the way to create sublime existence
is through the sublime world.

Wisdom can be collected from meaning,
creating the materials for sublime exis-

tence, permitting the sublime world and allowing the soul to realize itself through the neighbors, which are elements of the soul.

ET12

THE CORRELATION OF THE SUBLI-MATED HEAVENS

Inspired by the Greeks.

The cloud may look the same, and it is really the same. We have allegiance with the form of the cloud or we do not. Likewise, the cloud may look different. And here is the thing: we may be allied with Difference, or we may be allied with the cloud that is different.

So, in this way, it is really the same. Although, in another way, we know it may sometimes be a different cloud. And, we may love it or hate it, but we are allied with the Form or the Difference.

Now, let me speak of the form as the Same. This is not every cloud. It is the most rare cloud. It is the cloud that we love. And we ascribe many things to this cloud, although it is really just any cloud. This is the cloud we call the True Cloud. The highest form of the cloud, which we cannot always see.

And oftentimes, what we see is not the form of the same, but rather a different cloud. And, love it or hate it, it is not the same cloud. But still, we could love the cloud, or we could love the difference the cloud brings.

Now, let me speak of difference. Difference is true difference, but it is neither love nor hate. It is true that when we love what is different, it is not loving the same. It is a true difference. But, such it is true, we may hate it or we may love it.

Now, the True Difference is a different cloud, and it is not like the same. But we may hate it or we may love it. And we must know, it is truly a different love or hate, because it is a different thing, if for no other reason.

And it happens to be, the love of the different is completely different from the love of the same, for the different thing is of a

different nature if it is truly different, although it may truly be the same. And this
is what we call subtle.

But it happens to be the hatred of the same
and the different are really the same, they
are within us, and they are at opposition to
both the same and the different.

The clouds may be at war in the way of
clouds being different. They may be at war
about the same.

And we, being different from the clouds,
are not at war with the clouds. We are at
war with being different.

And now, it must be, if those who make
war are opposed to us, they are in love
with opposition, for they do not oppose
the clouds, nor do they oppose difference.

And so, if we are to have a soul, we must
make love with war, or embrace the same,
or fight the different.

And, fundamentally, it is the same-looking
clouds, one completely rare and familiar,
and the other completely common with
difference.

Where we fight, we must make love with war or fight the difference between all things. Everything else is the same like the clouds, and all of it is written in the form of clouds.

ET13

REALIZING ONE'S ULTIMATE POR-
POISE (SEE: REALIZING ONE'S ULTI-
MATE PORPOISE / EARLIER)

ET14

HAWKINGESQUE

But it's a small world if Nathan's not a genius. (A small world for him).

The dark coating on the wall is a Lorentz-permeate.

The features of the universe dance a dark dance.

Nothing is indestructible = a Neutron Star.

The perceptible medium is forever evading its ultimatums.

Toil without work will be information,
and an epiphany.

The touchstone of the future is the question of 'will we survive'.

It is not the same picture without certain
information.

The tension of the singularity is every-
where inside a black hole.

The history we make is not the same as the
history the universe makes.

At the end of the universe it will be time,
and cold, empty space.

The universe is not quite empty, because
there's entropy.

Black holes are like massive suns, that
never were suns.

The opposite of a sun is more powerful
than a sun, if only it were material.

ET15

A TASTE OF REAL-LIFE

1

The sight of the birds of paradise, and the peculiar call of those hunting them to extinction.

2

The knowledge Marie Antoinette had, of how to build a Cloissone egg, may have been the secret to perpetual motion.

3

Nothing can compare to visiting a vineyard. I think most can attest to that!

The authenticity! The beauty!

4

(Old man speaking)

Beautifully shaped, just like pears.

I was talking about pears, obviously.

The most beautiful pears!

ET16

THE GREAT UNDERSTANDINGS
(SEE THE GREAT UNDERSTANDINGS /
EARLIER)

ET17

PHILOSOPHY OF PARADISE

I think the one everyone is looking for is,
'How to live in paradise forever?'

Unfortunately not everyone is qualified, so
we are looking for 'How to justify paradise
in every possible way?'

'Is paradise what we want?'

'What will we do if we live there?'

'Does paradise need an ethical problem? Is
it ethical to live in paradise?'

'How can I find a more trustworthy paradise if that one c***s out on me? Maybe a conservative move with less risk-taking?'

'What can I do to make it easier for everyone to acquire paradise? For example, making art or writing poems, or designing something nifty with a computer?'

'What is the best paradise for me? A hot island, or cheap housing, or something more intellectual?'

'What can I do to live responsibly in paradise? Limit resource use?'

'What do I love most about paradise? Enjoyment?'

'If I have nightmares in paradise, how do I make the nightmares go away? By recovering past lives or improving yourself?'

'Does paradise improve over time? Does it have appeal and repeat value?'

'Am I already living in a kind of paradise? What if you have cookies and candy?'

'How to make the most of life in general?

Drag paradise around with you?'

'What do you say or think when you leave
paradise? Anything philosophical?'

'What is a paradise without paradise?
Drugs?'

'What is a paradise that isn't paradise?
Like Saltines, for instance?'

Originally posted here: What are the most
important, unanswered questions in metaphysics?

ET18

THE PSYCHOLOGICAL CONTINGENCY

Part of The Errata—

If someone is treated differently, one
should compensate for this in all future
dialogues.

Otherwise, be responsible for the effects
by changing the influence.

Or, work to create the right effects through

manipulation.

Or, exert charming manipulation.

Or educate them.

Or instruct them to follow a pattern.

Or bring them under control.

Or misinform them.

Or spy on them.

ET19

EXPLORING CHEMISTRY

1

A chemist said to me he could do everything, except he didn't know why his arms
were heavy. His arms had been heavy ever
since he learned chemistry.

I told him: "My best guess is your arms
are supposed to be cold, like non-
existent."

Thanks he said. It seemed to work to make his arms lighter.

What I didn't tell him was it was a reflection on antimatter. The equation for antimatter is summarized as 'the suns are relatively cold'.

2

Now if we want metaphysics we mix cold antimatter and sulfur, as sulfur represents potential metaphysics, and the cold antimatter will make it lighter and more plentiful.

If we then want it to do something we mix it with sodium, which produces potential processing. If we want consciousness to emerge in an unconfused way, we might first need calcium, which creates structure.

Then we might want carbon, magnesium, and potassium, for life, molecular compounds, and emotion respectively.

If we want advanced culture we will likely need chlorine for water processing, copper for change, zinc for transfer, phosphorous for ripening, and iron for seriousness.

3

The average chemist often solves things
volumetrically, but the first secret rule is
congregation by association:

Turmeric is good for the gut because of its
similarity to sulfur, the origin of the gut.

Likewise, sugar is good for the brain, as
sugar is similar in color to the bones,
which it is the brain's function to control.

We call this affinity.

Milk is largely responsible for male fertil-
ity, through its perpetuation of the bones
as a structure for the brain.

Aphrodisiacs like chocolate are passive-
reactive, reacting with the female system
through the craving for more, related to
the emotional attachment to pheremones
themselves attached to wielders of tools.

The immortal aspect then might be
guessed to be related to the internal wield-
ing of tools through imitation substances,

recreating a sexual function which aims to be perpetually self-justifying.

Where the internal is allied with mad anti-matter, it should seek complex smells, which provide ultimate knowledge. In this case survival will be a matter of interpretation.

Where the internal is allied with complex tools, it should seek internal sensation, priming the skeletal machine.

And thus, in some sense immortality begins as a combination of knowledge and machine, that is, smell and pleasure.

And it may be the ultimate cleverness at first to achieve that end without significant risk or hardship.

Now we can say that pain arrives primarily from deprivation of pleasure, and mad freedom is the power of thought, and so immortality emerges from the capacity for pleasure and thought, represented by technology and antimatter, antimatter being the force that can create lightness, and cause potential.

And thus the two powers are obsessional knowledge and prodigious plenty.

And their twins are fixate information and cultural authority.

4

Now the key for the immortality, if the soul is sulferic with antimatter may be either matter or anti-sulfur, for otherwise it has already attained knowledge and machine.

Likewise, if the soul is hormones and tools or pleasure and machine, it should seek out ultimately a lack of structure (anticalcium) or a lack of pleasure, or it is already fulfilled.

Thus, if pleasure is a machine, we get education and ignorance and immortality as exclusions.

If the soul is mad, the solution is elements or the avoidance of sulfur or immortality as exclusions.

Thus, the mad person should seek sulferic antimatter, representing interpretation, while the sane person must simply choose neither ignorance nor education, representing pleasure.

Granted, this is just a precis.

What is worth noting however is that further sucess of either type will likely depend on adding exponents (information or volumetrics), additional limited specialized reactions (such as drugs or genetics), or some combination of sanity and madness.

Thus, the madman might be expected to find pleasure, cure madness, adapt, or be perfect.

The sane person might be expected to react, go insane, adapt, or be perfect.

Thus, their realizations involve 4 parts pleasure from madness, 4 parts madness from sanity, 4 parts sanity from madness, 4 parts reaction, 8 parts adaptation, and 8 parts perfection.

Only 1/16 is two parts perfect, and only 1/16 is two parts adapted.

If we match the equal parts, then pleasure from madness is the reaction between sanity and insanity, and the measure of adaptation is what is perfect, and is only 1/2 likely.

So, now we conclude adaptation is random, and pleasure comes exclusively from complexity.

Now we could predict death is anticalcium, because calcium creates structure which is the basis for complexity, thus anticalcium is the destruction of structure, and the destruction of pleasure.

In effect, anticalcium is pain. This is a very natural view.

Now we know from much earlier that the pleasure machine is immortal, ignorant, or in pain. Thus, if immortal and pain are not ignorant, the immortal becomes knowledge of pleasure, represented by tools.

Thus, madness looks like a viable option if we have no pleasure. The madman either agrees that anticalcium is part of antimatter, or produces a partial reaction, or devotes himself to sulferic creativity.

Thus, the madman is a theoretical generalist who accepts the existence of pain, or a specialist against pain, or a creative person.

Now, there are only certain personalities of immortality if we are correct about sulfur, hormones, and similar parts being identical, and they are permutations of the immortal pleasure machine with the generalist, the specialist, and the creative.

Notice only the specialist sacrifices for pleasure.

Only the generalist acknowledges pain.

And only the creative completely reacts with antisulfur.

Thus, the artist is the creator, the generalist is the judge, and the specialist appears to bear responsibility.

Thus, from a wise alchemist's perspective, it is the specialist who bears risk and reaps reward, the generalist who learns, and the creative who acts. These seem to be the three Players of existence.

If there is a fourth player, it is the superficial I-Mage that wishes to do everything itself.

5.

At this point we might be prepared to see the immortal as a type of thought, re-affirming, reverberating, and re-constituting.

For the four personalities are really four chemical paradigms: the Generalist aims to become a living paradigm, the Specialist desires some type of special license, the Creative aims to achieve through action, and the I-Mage thrives on perfect art.

Thus, these are the personalities of immortality that are available: one glorifying immortal existence, another glorifying information, another glorifying heroism, and the last glorifying image.

These so to speak, are the metaphysical animals.

If immortality cannot be achieved by heroic, artistic, accredited existence, it might be unattainable.

The obvious thing to do is eliminate the dangers of existence through the proportions of properties found in the successful types.

Another, perhaps related approach is to find a formula, gene, drug, source of energy, etc that has the same effect as perfect adaptation.

6.

Inside a microscope is a little universe. Kind of literally. Things there have more scale.

Perhaps there was no universe before information theory.

The universe is constantly expanding from microscopic events. Changes in education if you will.

The whole project does not really have scale. What is interesting is what makes simple things difficult.

Perfection is what is difficult for complexity. With great power the entire universe is a small leap. Yet that leap is greater than any other.

The universe is made of significance and understanding. They do not combine well when they are neutral.

The universe must be perpetual and subtle, universal, and absolute. Therefore it is hard to have understanding.

Because understanding is difficult, it is the thing to focus on in the universe, if we know that everything matters to us.

But we do not always know, and so there are small events that break our consciousness. We cannot always focus on understanding. At times the universe is larger than us.

ET20

TRUTH RATIONALISM

The success of the soul is its proof, negation-refuting and self-affirming, self-proving.

The universal is its source, which is also infinite, and in its folded nature convinces nature of a higher precept than nature, which in truth is any good thing.

For what is good is what is true, and what is evil, by the deliberation of proof, is false.

And so, the evilest things are merely the things that resist proof.

And the truth is set higher than deliberation.

And what is higher than some truth is merely double-truth, which is higher truth.

ET21

EXPLORING PHYSICS (SEE PHYSICS EARLIER)

ET22

THE GREEN MAN

The green man really has sex, that is one
theory.

The green man is like a masturbator god,
that is another theory.

The green man made an infinite sacrifice.

"The green man is the counterweight of
God" : that is a green man idea.

The green man is highly intelligent.

But the green man's intelligence only ap-
plies to certain areas.

The green man is decorated with souls.

And the green man has his eye on the just
sacrifice.

The green man is the counterweight of
God.

The green man is a handsome simpleton to
women.

ET23

THE ORACLE

Will I get hurt? Maybe not, maybe it is a friendly meeting.

Will I live to see another day? Things will happen as usual.

Have I offended him? His conscience is clear.

When will it happen? In its due time, or not at all.

When can I expect love in return? When you have spent yourself completely.

What can I expect of the new arrangement? A successful failure.

How do I achieve great things? Do not look very far.

What is the wisest principle? If you are brave, do what you were meant to do. Otherwise, keep to yourself, and do not expect anything.

How do I make a great life? Persist, and you may have to miss the boat many times.

What is left for me? Nothing is truly different. Life is as it was. Evil is evil, and good is good.

When will my luck change? It will change when you try your best.

How do I know what to do? Try everything, or give up and hope for the best. Then, try harder, and focus on only one thing.

What can you teach me? I can teach you: you are beginning to know everything about what you already knew would happen.

How can I improve? Its not a riddle, you know your own ability: experience it, and you will know much more about it. Relative to now, your ability will be perfect.

What is the answer? The answer is what you make of it.

What is the meaning of life? Stranger

things have happened, and we have made less of it. What is more, life has more meaning than that, and it is rare.

ET24

MYERS-BRIGGS NIRVANA

The first secret of introverts is that they're crazy. The second secret of introverts is that they're geniuses.

The first secret of extroverts is that they live in the universe. The second secret is that other people can be explained.

The first secret of intuition is meaning. The second secret of intuition is understand-ing.

The first secret of sensory is that you lose. The second secret of sensory is that you win.

The first secret of feeling is happiness. The second secret of feeling is that imagination is love is God.

The first secret of thinking is that they live inside their heads. The second secret of thinking is that they have power.

The first secret of perception is fascination with interesting things. The second secret is dimensional.

The first secret of judgment is discernment. The second secret is good judgment.

Maybe history is just seeing in front of my eyes.

I've done too much to achieve nirvana.

I'm realizing how subjectivity has scale.

You should know that Myers-Briggs nirvana is worth a joke at least.

That's the logic!

ET25

INTUITIVE CHINESE: LATER

HOW TO BE SMART #15

1

Remember the important parts.

Make a list of the parts that are most complex and hardest to remember in abbreviated format.

Now, assuming you have basic knowledge of the subject, studying the complex parts until you have key intuitions about them will help greatly for your exam.

2

Study more intensively (on the parts that are important).

3

Develop networks of association.

Remember patterns in association.

4

Keep an active memory.

…

HOW TO BE SMART #16

INTUITIVE CHINESE

Note: this is a strange, alternate system
you are not likely to learn in school.

BASIC CHARACTER TYPES

上 and similar means money or 'for sure'.
The similar 正 means thesis or 'I think'.
The unusual character 忙 means 'formal'
or 'official'.

可 means bureaucracy, which is important
in China.

业 and similar is a basic version of 'fuck',
成 and 候 also mean fuck. 的 and 时 mean
fucked all around.

本 means shit. If the lower bar is higher
like this: 来, it means body.

Similarly, 也 and 他 means business.

以 means woman. 课 means fine woman.
These are common characters.

145

财 means something like teacher.

吃 probably means doing it.

发 means whore, so it means 'try'.

EXCEPTIONAL CHARACTERS TO
WATCH OUT FOR

So far as I know, 完 means bomb.

过 means charm, handsome, and its literal
meaning is 'the face of a man'.

作 and 们 so far as I know means holy or
erudite.

Complex characters generally mean immortal. 舅 means super-immortal, which
means your relative. 舅舅 means relative
of your relative.

Characters like 挣 and 钱 also mean immortal.

能 is complicated but distinct, so it means

complicated.

ADDITIONAL CHARACTERS

Slash to the left, like: 有 means spirit, school, emperor's chop-mark.

Slashes underneath, like: 些 means the end, general feeling.

CHARACTERS CONSIDERED COMPLI-CATED

着 means value because it means immortal school.

PREDICTION ABILITY

I translated "Uncles should make money when they grow up" as "My elite business thesis is about formal values".

I translated "School is over, I should write down my homework, too" as "I like my fucking professor."

ADVANCED CHINESE

Chinese is a vertical language. It has many nuances which are not immediately necessary. This was the original idea of how to learn language rapidly.

RUMORS:

The less you practice the better you are at Chinese.

Note: For thoughts leading up to this, see: Enlightened Thinking

149

HOW TO BE SMART #17

COGNITIVE SCIENCE HEURISTICS

1. Help with [Quality] or something.

HOW TO BE SMART #18

THE WAY OF LIFE

In my case you have an embarrassing set of ears, a mental illness, not a lot of money, and are trying to change the world with ideas.

Someone else might be married, with venereal diseases, an average appearance, and a lot of debt from mortgages and paying for cars. They're not sure they can hold onto their marriage, but they love their affair or their kids or their job.

Someone else might be trying to cover up that their job as a lawyer is a sham and they have a heavy drinking problrm and are depressed and a loner, and they look sort of ugly but respectable.

Some other people look perfect but don't really do much intellectual or they are miserable but very attractive and make a good impression on others and they develop a drug problem or obesity or work out and have bad sex experiences or die young.

There are some people who escape the system at least temporarily, but they tend to be attractive people who are good with money who don't have much fun, or health nuts, neurotic people, or people who have struggled very hard.

You may need to be more neurotic. Just say you don't care anymore. You don't give a shit anymore. Who could disprove that?

Or you may need to pitch in, and learn you can do more than your share of hard work. Its not your fault if they can't do it.

Or, maybe you know you have the gold ticket. You were gifted, and have nothing to prove. All you need is healthy living.

Or, you're looking for an edge and will do anything. Well, if you're attractive and don't need to have fun, all you need is to be good with money.

Otherwise than these four, its back to ordinary problems, which tend to hurt.

HOW TO BE SMART #19

"COMMON MAN": THE REVELATION OF THE MYSTERY OF (RAPE)

Judge: "What are you here for?"

Offendant: "Rape."

Judge: "Well, what do you say?"

Offendant: "I'm sorry!! Why did my penis fall off?"

Judge: "You offended God. Now, your penis might grow back. Well, did it?"

Offendant: "Oh!!! Yes!! Why did she burn my penis off?"

Judge: "Because she is God."

Offendant: "Ah, I see! God created me, and in the demented logic, I look similar to God."

HOW TO BE SMART #20

HUMILITY

Am I gifted? Of course not, I haven't been telling jokes about the meaning of life!

Atheism? I learned my lesson!

Lightning? I don't know the language!

Women? God help me!

HOW TO BE SMART #21
ARROGANCE

It still seems like Wisdom is the ultimate achievement.

That's not very reassuring.

Maybe Wisdom is the Babel of Wisdom to God.

Maybe someone powerful thinks history is a marching of the fools.

Then why seek wisdom of any kind?

But we know it is an ultimate achievement.

But we are arrogant to think it is the acheivement of God!

And we are arrogant to wait!

And if we are not wise, we are arrogant to know about other fools!

Maybe we should consider God before

Wisdom, Babel before history, and woman before man!

What is left of the foolish quest?

Is not 'God' instead diabolical temptation?

What would a fool even think?

And therefore, how can we ever know are wise?

And therefore, who are we to question the Wisdom of God?

Silence is well spoken on these matters of knowledge—nature may have hidden depth—and much account is made of nothing.

Who are we to plumb the depths of nature?

What if this exploration is its only death?

And yet, who are we to know that nature is perfect?

And who are we to know the perfect Creation?

If what is desired is emotion, there is emotion enough in terror and the revelation of beauty—an emotion somewhat more powerful than any foolish pretended wisdom!

Yet, is this emotion what is meant by revelation—or by understanding? Far from it!

For although man might know God by her Creation, he will not know the Babel of God, nor will he know the emotion of Truth Wisdom.

For these things are not the depth of nature, nor are they foolish pretended wisdom.

Therefore, although Wisdom begins with the Babel of God, it does not end with it, nor can we consider man's wisdom anything that man does not know.

For, although it may be medieval temptation, man may be wise to avoid it, and the spirit of man's wisdom will be the wisdom of man.

Whether God hates and reviles him, or considers him a work of nature, his wisdom is only God if it is with God, and his wisdom is only of Nature if it is with Nature.

Therefore, God may be Nature with or without Man, and Man may encounter Nature that is or is not wise.

But it seems true to accounts that whether or not Man encounters God, he is Wise to avoid medieval temptation.

And so, Man should avoid Woman, and so he should avoid God, but he should not avoid Nature or Wisdom.

Therefore Man is best made a devil in the image of woman, just as woman is made in image of God. But Man is a philosopher, not a creator, and his wisdom is the wisdom of fools, and avoiding temptation.

Where there is creation however, Man is not likely a devil, as Nature is evil, and metaphysics is woman.

Therefore Man should seek foolish philosophy, and abandon creation, and dwell on his own derivatives of woman. For Nature is corrupt, and God is unbearable and

157

far from Man. God is not the cure, nor is woman. Nor is philosophy wise. The honest struggle begins with humility, and the death of temptation, and the absolvement of sin.

Man was never a sinner, but rather a fool, and a lover of careless wisdom. It was the wisdom of fools, not the wisdom of God, nor was it the wisdom of creation. Man must abandon the Truth of the metaphysics of woman and adopt the wisdom of fools.

Then his tongue will be freed and he will know his own creation, not of God or woman, but of philosophical fools. Not creators, judgers, or destroyers, but mere enjoyers of appearance, fancy, and curiosity.

In this subtle place that Man imagines, he is free from folly and from judgment. Such a world will be ruled by desire that is passionless and empty. Everything will be provided by ideas at the utmost expense. It will be a world that means nothing to God the creator—a bauble, an enjoyment, not serious. To Man this just means it is not a temptation, not a creation. It is a different metaphysics, the metaphysics of the survival of man. Humble wisdom, foolish philosophy.

Nothing is left of judgment for Man. He is proven a fool, and this is his victory. For his success was never judgment, and his thought is not of woman's creation, but rather of foolish philosophy.

In the wisdom of humility lives on the creation of man. True love, much unlike God and woman.

HOW TO BE SMART #22
HOW TO THINK LIKE BRIAN COPPEDGE

Divide the board. Put the best thing in each square. Treat the squares as equal, with equal weight. Improve the squares. Improve knowledge. Make new squares.

Don't get me wrong… it might be more advanced than Chinese…

For example,

1.

Virtuous writings—Writings that concern special valuable topics that explain values.

Satya—A meaning I associate with certain writings that have the quality of extreme depth and also somewhat off-the-cuff. Alternately, it can also mean writings that are honest about the world's evils, or writings derived from authentic meditation.

2.

Arrogance

It still seems like Wisdom is the ultimate
achievement.

That's not very reassuring.

Maybe Wisdom is the Babel of Wisdom to
God.

Maybe someone powerful thinks history is
a marching of the fools.

Then why seek wisdom of any kind?

But we know it is an ultimate achievement.

But we are arrogant to think it is the
acheivement of God!

And we are arrogant to wait!

And if we are not wise, we are arrogant to
know about other fools!

Maybe we should consider God before

Wisdom, Babel before history, and woman before man!

What is left of the foolish quest?

Is not 'God' instead diabolical temptation?

What would a fool even think?

And therefore, how can we ever know are wise?

And therefore, who are we to question the Wisdom of God?

Silence is well spoken on these matters of knowledge—nature may have hidden depth—and much account is made of nothing.

Who are we to plumb the depths of nature?

What if this exploration is its only death?

And yet, who are we to know that nature is perfect?

And who are we to know the perfect Creation?

If what is desired is emotion, there is emotion enough in terror and the revelation of beauty — an emotion somewhat more powerful than any foolish pretended wisdom!

Yet, is this emotion what is meant by revelation — or by understanding? Far from it!

For although man might know God by her Creation, he will not know the Babel of God, nor will he know the emotion of Truth Wisdom.

For these things are not the depth of nature, nor are they foolish pretended wisdom.

Therefore, although Wisdom begins with the Babel of God, it does not end with it, nor can we consider man's wisdom anything that man does not know.

For, although it may be medieval temptation, man may be wise to avoid it, and the spirit of man's wisdom will be the wisdom of man.

Whether God hates and reviles him, or considers him a work of nature, his wisdom is only God if it is with God, and his wisdom is only of Nature if it is with Nature.

Therefore, God may be Nature with or without Man, and Man may encounter Nature that is or is not wise.

But it seems true to accounts that whether or not Man encounters God, he is Wise to avoid medieval temptation.

And so, Man should avoid Woman, and so he should avoid God, but he should not avoid Nature or Wisdom.

Therefore Man is best made a devil in the image of woman, just as woman is made in image of God. But Man is a philosopher, not a creator, and his wisdom is the wisdom of fools, and avoiding temptation.

Where there is creation however, Man is not likely a devil, as Nature is evil, and metaphysics is woman.

Therefore Man should seek foolish philosophy, and abandon creation, and dwell on his own derivatives of woman. For Nature is corrupt, and God is unbearable and far from Man. God is not the cure, nor is woman. Nor is philosophy wise. The honest struggle begins with humility, and the death of temptation, and the absolvement of sin.

Man was never a sinner, but rather a fool, and a lover of careless wisdom. It was the wisdom of fools, not the wisdom of God, nor was it the wisdom of creation. Man must abandon the Truth of the metaphysics of woman and adopt the wisdom of fools.

Then his tongue will be freed and he will know his own creation, not of God or woman, but of philosophical fools. Not creators, judgers, or destroyers, but mere enjoyers of appearance, fancy, and curiosity.

In this subtle place that Man imagines, he is free from folly and from judgment. Such a world will be ruled by desire that is passionless and empty. Everything will be provided by ideas at the utmost expense. It will be a world that means nothing to God the creator—a bauble, an enjoyment, not serious. To Man this just means it is not a temptation, not a creation. It is a different metaphysics, the metaphysics of the survival of man. Humble wisdom, foolish philosophy.

Nothing is left of judgment for Man. He is proven a fool, and this is his victory. For his success was never judgment, and his thought is not of woman's creation, but rather of foolish philosophy.

In the wisdom of humility lives on the creation of man. True love, much unlike God and woman.

3.

Miscellaneous Psychic Inferences

Divided line variation: if one thing is good, good things can be added to it until complete good is achieved.

Finite distance: some small change occurs over time. It matters how small it is.

4.

Rape…

The judge must have been very pretty…

(It explains everything about illegal sex…
A compulsion outside itself, involving a
third figure, serving as surrogate for the
first. Or, on a deeper level, rape is the creation of a wrathful woman who is God, and
so, since the rapist does not desire this, he
must desire some further thing that comes
from judgment… he must desire a female
judge… and since he desires her, she must
be sexy… and so, he must be stupid, even
if he is a rapist).

5.

Its amazing the luck I'd need to survive
schizophrenia…

Of course, it would be wasted, on surviv-
ing schizophrenia…

6.

Adventure Logic

Everyone is trying to do the same thing if
they are the same character.

If there's only one good character, then
everything stays the same.

Sometimes they miss something and they
go into a special area.

And if they are legend, a miracle happens.

And if they are unfortunate, they die from
a deadfall trap.

What is left is a miracle, or destruction.

Only in this way can we reason about possibility, unless we have logic locked up.

Here is the secret: the devils know calculus and Chinese, and sometimes opening the wrong treasure is a deadly trap.

7.

Brian and Deepness

Brian: Nathan, where are you?

Nathan: In the kiddie pool! I like it here!

Brian: Deep!!

Nathan: No!!

Brian: DEEP!!!

Nathan: NO-O!!!!

Brian: Come to the deep side!

Nathan: I think I'll just read my book.

Brian: You can't read it in the kiddie pool.

Nathan: Why not? Well, I don't want to go over to the deepside. I'm against swimming.

Michael: Well, its sink or swim!

Nathan: NO-o!!

Brian: I knew you'd say that!

8.

Magic

Formal questions trump all, because we owe a debt of gratitude to these people no one could hope to understand.

There's chaos with the right answers, someone's trying to claim.

Magic is the logos: religion doesn't have it, and science ignores it.

The beauty of location is to become a time-traveler.

Many powers are great that have local

time importance.

Trickery is subtle, and beneath the gods.

Athena knows best is the subtlest secret
that only Athena knows, but knowing this,
we know more than most.

9.

The Functionalities:

Soul

It has ancient pedigree.

Try an artform.

Maybe you'll grow!

Transcend onto a higher path!

Body

Handle business.

Get on a level playing field.

Chemistry! Go for it!

If you are wise, you may live on a high plateau.

Abstract

Do some processing.

There are standards—of responsibility, for example.

Know your limits.

Make a place for yourself within the social hive.

...

HOW TO BE SMART #23

EMOTIONAL BRAIN BOOSTING

EBB1
THE PSYCHOLOGICAL CONTINGENCY

Part of The Errata —

If someone is treated differently, one should compensate for this in all future dialogues.

Otherwise, be responsible for the effects by changing the influence.

Or, work to create the right effects through manipulation.

Or, exert charming manipulation.

Or educate them.

Or instruct them to follow a pattern.

Or bring them under control.

Or misinform them.

Or spy on them.

EBB2
ON TRANSITIVITY

There is a sense that what is upside-down
emerges from balance.

—We are all born, we all work, we all get
sick, we all die—

But What If?

What if we WERE immortal, or if death
had no meaning? If life were not a struggle?

Would it mean the same thing? Would
anything change? Would life be just a feeling?

Now, we might wonder if life is a closed
system under illusion: where is life's limit
if it is defined arbitrarily?

Who lives and who dies in any given moment?

And, is there any reason to human nature?

Well, as a rule, let us not trespass too far,
but instead keep firm knowledge of our
domain—

For surely if we do not learn all there is of
where we are, we will never travel very
far—

Like the man who returns to his home
town only to discover that everything he
once knew is gone—!

That is not really learning.

Then there is also a vision of a whole life—

One theory is, life begins with ideas!

If you have a closed system, you might
still need a key, and once you have a key
you may still have to use it—

So, life is not so different from a perpetual
motion machine.

EBB3
WEIRD WORLD

Starting with terms based on kind-of puns.

The Dennist: Somewhere there is a guy named Dennist that unconsciously works as a dentist.

Graves' Humurus: If someone named Graves is buried, then graves humor may exist in the grave.

The Holy Boog: There may be a booger way out in outer space that could not have gotten there with any amount of rocket fuel. In effect, the 'boog' is holier than the Book. This can be used as an argument for having more than one holy book, and including real facts.

Money R: In a certain world, money is only an idea.

New-paper: In a certain world a newspaper is an unexplained event that is forgotten when it disappears.

A Poser's Proem: May be a prose poem.

Then they own your ear.

Treeth: In one place, the the truth is a tree, and everything surrounding it is explained through it. None of it would be real without the tree.

EBB4
PURE RELAXATION

Pretty great. Pretty good.

Pretty great. Wait. Pretty good. Breathe.

Chill. Wait it out. Relax.

2

Take a chill pill.

Wait what seems like forever.

De-stress.

Fold your arms over your chest.

Breathe.

Lift up your arms.

Breathe out.

Lie down comfortably.

Measure some seconds.

The whole Earth is chilling out.

Laugh.

3

Shake your arms out.

Take a chill pill.

Think of something that comforts you.

De-stress.

Move your arms.

Feel that you are gaining some control.

Notice your third eye, if you have one.

Tell your third eye to relax.

Move your hands and fingers around.

Get in touch with your inner child.

Relax.

4

Find a quiet space.

Breathe deeply.

Silence has a soul.

Give yourself to the moment.

Find your peace.

There is wisdom in this silence.

EBB5

MORALITY ANTICIPATING THE BEI-TRÄGE

The Beiträge (Bi-Tray-Guh) is a later work of Heidegger's that possibly only exists in German. I have been unable to find an English translation.

However, my professor DP has bern giving hints that the Beiträge is a later work of Heidegger's where much of his vocabulary is found, if it is not found in Being and Time, A Letter on Humanism, or The Origin of the Work of Art, and that the work sounds Buddhist to some ears.

At first, there is a certain way of action.

First, it involves ritual. Then, it involves art. Then it involves thought. And, then it involves the transcendental.

Then, we might move on and pursue the same things differently and more spiritually, and even sometimes do things differently.

When it takes place—when actions fall into a form—we wonder, though, what happened, not whether it is good or bad as much as that IT IS.

Although truly good and bad could be remarkable facts, they are contained by the life of the thing that worlds.

Therefore it must be important to find that thing, which is the cause of being, as well as the deep correspondingness that precedes Being.

Even so, the art of being is not its heart, for while being has a form, it is not the essence or essence of the form that would be its heart.

That is, unless being is only a work of art. Far from making that kind of declension, it must be resolved that the heart corresponds, and only when it corresponds directly is Being the same as art.

In other cases, there is a certain 'indirection' to the nature of Being, unless, that is, nature is only restricted to the heart, and not the entire nature of being.

Therefore, nature is restricted, or Being
has indirection, or Being is the same thing
as art.

Correlation is seen to be art, so causal nature is only unrestricted when its nature is
indirect. Therefore the entire picture is of a
nature that is unrestricted except for the
restraint of art.

Therefore we must conclude that art is re-
strained so far as its limit, which lies well
beyond the heart of being, but the undeter-
mined limit is the heart, and at the same
time only indirectly corresponding with
the truth of Being.

Therefore, the heart of being is a feeling,
while art is the correspondence, and being
is the indirect correlation.

Essence then, is the passive, fixed art
which underlies causal nature. Essence is
the tool of Being. True nature is unques-
tioned when it is contested.

Out of essential art comes timeless movement, which is merely thought. Correlation is the changeless cause of difference in
Being. Thought emerges from thought in

the manner that essence does not change.

Without a manner of acting, the changeless relies on essential correspondence and
indirect Being.

With a manner of acting, Being comes
from strife and indirectness.

If correspondence is strife, and indirectness means indirect being, then there is no
difference between acting and non-acting.
All is caught on the essential art of corre-
spondingation.

HOW TO BE SMART #24
ALIEN LOGIC

1.

S.

General.

Strings.

Logic.

Rules.

…

2.

IIIQ

I haven't really proved I'm wrong.

If that's really true:

I'm right!

Q
…

HOW TO BE SMART #25

THE SECRETS OF THE SOLAR SYS-TEM

TSOTSS1

Note: this theory has been somewhat dis-proved by observing that Atomic Number 9 is actually Fleurine, and 6 is Carbon.

1

The Sun looks like the nucleus of an atom.

Atoms have a nucleus that is surrounded by neutrons and protons.

Planets and moons have neutral energy, like neutrons.

The Earth has nine planets.

Carbon = Atomic Number 9.

Humans are carbon-based lifeforms.

Therefore, we know the solar system has nine planets.

Objectively, the types of solar systems are described by the periodic table.

Omniscient knowledge may be had by combining causality and the periodic table.

If we know humans are carbon-based life-forms, we can also guess that the solar system has nine planets.

If things are as they appear, consciousness of each element appears where the number of planets is equal to the number of neutrons in the corresponding type of atom.

We know this based on the assumption that a solar system is an atom. And perhaps this idea is why you may not have been allowed to look inside an electron microscope.

However, we further know this because according to one physics prof, subatomic particles (which are much smaller than neutrons) are actually not much smaller than humans when they manifest, although their information properties can be observed easily under certain conditions with a powerful microscope.

For example, in a very rare divine event, I observed a Higgs Boson appear once in a dark room. It was basketball-sized, and the center was somewhat dark, with a semi-transparent sphere around it. It appeared for only perhaps 1.2 seconds before vanishing, not enough time to photograph it. When it appeared, I could not really deny that it was God or God's creation. It seems that when something is really real, there is a tendency to not be able to deny any of the characteristics of what it really is. And so, what is real about the God Particle happens to be that it is God or God's Creation. At least, that is the thing that is real about it, and that is the real impression it makes.

So now, based on this observation of the God Particle and the observation of neutral spheres around a very large nucleus, we can interpret that a solar system or atom with nine planets or neutrons has atomic number 9, and therefore is an example of a carbon-based world.

Clearly other solar systems do exist, which

because of the properties of atoms which correspond to their nucleus, have the form of consciousness which corresponds to their particular atomic element.

2

If a carbon atom dies it might be through loss of energy, which sounds like radiation.

More complex atoms might have more intense radiation, and give off what might be considered more complex energy.

If we are part of carbon, this energy would be analogous to much higher intelligence.

The radioactive equivalent of a carbon atom that most people think of is Carbon-14.

If Carbon-14 expresses the maximum lifetime of Carbon, it could be used to describe the maximal lifetime of Carbon solar systems.

Expressed in terms of subatomic particles for example, the survival rate of the solar system might be only 12.5% every 17,000 years like a piece of wood. However, in fact, there may be something more universal about Carbon than its Carbon element, which creates longer motions for the overall system.

In this sense the radioactive element is actually the life of the atom, because it has more perdurance than the simple concept of atomic motion, except in a vacuum.

TSOTSS2 (Ignore as desired)

1. If Marie Antoinette created Pluto as I remember, then there may be fewer than 9 planets.

2. Then there really might be six, in which case it may still be a carbon solar system.

3. Mercury might be fake (humans seem to own the solar system and are not very tricky).

4. Now we can predict that the Earth is the 2nd rock from the Sun.

5. This makes sense in the roleplaying version of the universe where a goddess

might be given two dimensional rings
(two rocks / two diamonds) to grow her
breasts. Some truths might be unavoid-
able.

6. It might also explain how humanity is
known for inventing the toilet and using
dirty language.

TSOTSS3 (Ignore as desired)

1. The thought of the dimensional world
was first kept in a young man's diary.

2. Di-tit-mensional-arie. Rumored to be a
screaming book, although the scream was
just an abstraction.

3. Anyway, the diary was original, and
motivated by virtue, but it was an objecti-
fication, and so, it was a cursed book, like
the book of a little girl.

4. If the book captivated a man, it was just
as true that the queen did not know how
to touch anyone. And so it seemed, the
book was not so cursed, and really contained virtue, maybe even everything. For,
in some ways it contained all the virtue of

someone who knew all the magic of the dimensional rings.

5. Fool! Someone says. But are they trying to cast a spell? Is it a coincidence that its precisely what I have to know? Indeed, the book could contain virtues, and yet virtues are greater than a fool, and so it must be something great to hear as you already know! Its an honest magical book, just reduced to shadows and simplicity.

6. It is indeed the 2nd World, captivated by its own shitty book, a world dominated by a large-breasted queen with two dimensional rings.

7. Maybe only a 'people', born among such things, would hear the word 'diarrhea' and take faith.

8. Thus, the religion of unlucky people is not as religious as the lucky religion, although it might be predicted to become religious. Even so, the complexity found with luck is not the same as the unlucky complexity, and there is virtue in both, even while there is also success in neither.

HOW TO BE SMART #26
IMPISH LANGUAGE

Q&A:
Q: Are you (smart)?
A: Maybe I am too.
Q: Let's buy groceries.
A: Is that all?
Q: I've noticed you sound like Brian
David.
A: Don't we stand tall?

Inventiveness:

What is a bee's nest?
A horn's rest.

Who's your leader?
No one more important than me.

Themes:

Independence, unexpected intelligence.

HOW TO BE SMART #27

THE HIGH PLATEAU

THP1
INTELLIGENCE CONTEST

1. I have knowledge.

2. I can solve paradoxes.

3. I am a student in psychology.

4. I know my limits.

5. I know about physics.

6. I know some basic things about quantum mechanics.

7. I have studied human anatomy.

8. I know about chemistry.

9. I know Chinese.

10. I understood rape when I was 7 years old.

11. Atoms—subatomic particles, I mean, are larger than you think.

12. You may not know that this is a carbon -based solar system.

13. Einstein knew more about biology than you would admit. Radioactivity or atomic energy is a biological theory of death and immortal life.

14. I know nothing.

THP2
DIASCARRI: THE DANCE WITH DARK-NESS

Finding darkness…

The art of finding darkness when you shut your eyes…

Maybe the only spiritual prize.

Brilliance may be unwise.

Intelligence, technology: Am I feeding God or Socrates to the fish?

Turn right turn left a little, stare up…

Did it get darker?

Turn right some more.

Turn a corner.

Stare into the relatively dark ceiling.

Sometimes this is as dark as it gets.

Should I really escape brilliance to find
meaning?

Doesn't this mean I won't fall in love?

But isn't it the obvious choice?

Wasn't I perfect when all was darkness?

Was it not the meaning of life?

How do I reclaim my darkness?

My sanity?

The palace without the dancer?

THP3
DEEP ETHICS

The blind horse is the good horse.

When talking to the gods, 'Perfect lie' is a deception, but that doesn't mean its a lie…

What if rationality is a big boon?

Practical happiness prospers, practical prosperity withers.

Enjoy the culture of withering or prospering by happiness.

Now you know that the lie of 'meet your doom' is love on the line.

THP4
MICHAEL'S NEGATIVE PREDICTOR

Michael made predictions about his two sons.

He thought: Brian is smart and pessimistic, so something will happen to him, probably something smart and wonderful.

Then he thought: Nathan is not so smart, and expects everything to go well, so maybe something terrible will happen to Nathan.

So, he went around his business expecting something awful to happen to Nathan, and something wonderful to happen to Brian.

As the years went on, Nathan developed a mental illness, and Brian fell in love. And Michael thought, this is not so different than what I expected.

But, is mental illness really that bad? Nathan is taken care of by the government, and Brian's love relationship did not turn out perfect. Its time to revise expectations.

Nathan was optimistic about intelligence, and intelligence alone. Brian was pessimistic about love, and optimistic about college.

Now probably it will comtinue, but things will get better in the areas where they were worse, and worse in areas where they were fine. That's what happens when you're smart.

And it seemed like, Nathan's mental health was improving, but college cost a lot of money. Brian's love relationship failed, but he was still friends with his ex-girlfriend.

Things seemed to go as predicted! It just happens to depend on the model!

THP5
THE SUBTLE MEDICINE

1. Open your eyes. The world will not mistake you.

2. Look up to your betters. This way you will have wisdom.

3. Make time into an account. You will live long.

4. Apply a cooling balm. The way may open.

5. Practice transfiguration. Time may pass.

6. Apply a slight pressure. You might live to 148.

THP6
IRONIC KNOWLEDGE

You can answer any really dumb question with a random but interesting answer, as long as you don't get locked in an insane asylum.

Average questions can be answered with different categories of expert knowledge—collect them all.

Particular more expert queries can be answered by being fascinating and justifying satisfaction. When the experts are satisfied, this is what most people mean by finding the answer.

Extremely esoteric queries are solved by developing an object of fascination which is designed to evoke answers which fit the asker's mentality. As long as the larger group of objects holds together, the world seems to 'make sense'.

HOW TO BE SMART #28

ABSTRACT POLYPS

A dragon is not a polyp.

A polyp is more neutral than a dragon.

A polyp is substantially neutral.

Multiple polyps can have common texts,
and common cultures.

What relates polyps is held in common
with other relations.

A polyp remains neutral.

Although, by terms of polyps some relations may have identity.

Outside of a polyp the relation may be
neutral.

Inside the relation of polyps, the interrela-
tion may look weighted.

The polyps are neutral weighted relations.

The culture of polyps is the culture or text of neutral weighted relations.

The polyp-text or culture may be real by terms of its external relation.

Although internally neutral, the polyp culture can have an external texture.

Although abstract, the polyp-text is not ideal. This defines its external relation.

The boundary of its external relation is neuther ideal nor non-ideal.

Through this paradigm, one might predict an endless series of co-relations.

However, the outside series may have a limit. This defines the internal of the outside boundary.

There is also a place in which boumdaries are unlimited, defined by the extension of the purportedly limited boundary.

In one place the boundary is unbounded and unlimited, in another place the extension might demand a second polyp-text.

The second polyp-text, however, is just as important as no such second polyp-text.

Therefore, the relation between texts or cultures is just as important as the disrelation.

So, in the sense that it is not a dragon, an abstract polyp-culture might require an important unimportant relation, or a finite infinite relation.

Also keep in mind that these relations occur on the boundary of the polyp.

Internally, the polyp remains neutral, is sometimes weighted, and exists as a text.

However, we may note some things about weighted relations.

The weight of any one polyp may be the weight of the others: in effect only one polyp may have weight, although this may be determined by the relations, e.g. the weightedness may reflect on the important unimportant and finite infinite relations.

One may ask if the polyps define a closed-yet-significant logic or if some defined logic lies outside of the boundary of all polyp-text.

Indeed, the boundary of polyp-texts has an internal boundary co-relation. The internal logic is limited by that boundary, by the polyp-text co-relation, and by the inflection internal to that boundary.

The boundary may, however, be external to the polyps, although it may not be external to the weight of the polyps.

But, would we assume polyps have weight?

Indeed, the logic of co-relation may be external to the weight of a boundary. If we do not assume the boundary has weight, polyps become exceptional disrelations the boundary of which may still have an internal logic.

Now, let us assume polyps have weight.

We may assume the internal boundary co-relation between texts is weighted, except just as easily it is unweighted, although it seems if it had weight it would be the weight of the internal co-relation, that is, the weight of the internal boundary.

There are several options here, all concern the inflection. The inflection may have the special weight of the polyp, which is an inflected co-relation between polyps. Or, the inflection may inflect polyps without a co-relation. Or, the inflection may be disposable, like a deflected external.

Although not bearing on internal relations, the simplest answer here is the deflected external, which places the prior-mentioned inflected boundary on par with infinite co-relations with externals.

Now there is a direct co-relation between internal polyps and infinity, through the inflected boundary or inflected co-relations.

We have yet to talk of external polyps.

One possibility is an infinite polyp which summarizes co-relations within some hyper-polyp-text, in which case the co-relation may be infinite, with an infinite hyper-inflected boundary.

Another possibility is that the external polyp is the same as internal polyps, in which case the possibility is an express co-co-relation of boundaries, and internal co-co-relation of inflected co-relations.

A third possibility is that the external polyps have indefinite or variant scale, in which case the relation is by internal weight of the boundary and its co-variations. In this case external co-relations might be defined by a further hyper-co-inflected boundary inflected within the first inflected boundary.

Now that we have taken a tour of internal and external polyps, there are a few things worth noting:

1. Polyps are defined internally through inflected co-relations (the internal boundary of a single polyp).

2. The boundary is hyper-inflected (boundaries in general are co-inflected with infinity or have disrelation).

3. Any given polyp-text is internally inflected, with no necessary external inflection. This means that although the logic

may relate externally, true external co-relations do not exist without some form of express extro-flection. Thus, there is a key difference between internal and external boundaries of polyps.

I HOPE YOU HAVE ENJOYED THIS—

THERE ARE POSSIBLE EXPANSIONS ON FUTURE PRINTINGS...

OTHER
RECOMMENDED READING
BY NATHAN COPPEDGE

The Book of Ideas

Programmable Heuristics

The Dimensional Philosopher's
Toolkit

BIO—

Nathan Coppedge Is a philosopher, artist, inventor, and poet in some capacity, and a member of the International Honor Society for Philosophers. He lives in New Haven near Yale University.

210

www.ingramcontent.com/pod-product-compliance
Lightning Source LLC
Chambersburg PA
CBHW050908260726
48660CB00001B/93